# T·E·A·M
# SPONSORING

# T·E·A·M
# SPONSORING

# O.J. BRYSON,
## B.A., M.M., D.M.A.

Fleming H. Revell Company
Old Tappan, New Jersey

11-7-00

ISBN 0-8007-5263-5l

**Logo © 1987 O.J. Bryson**

# Contents

# Recapitulation

## Pastoral Symphony

## Coda

## Postlude

# Acknowledgments

How can I say thanks? Here is my best effort. I would like to say thanks to my sponsors, H. A. and Barbara Sessions, who taught me traditional network marketing concepts. Chuck and Jeanne Strehli, my Crown Ambassadors, having become believers, walked beside me where angels feared to tread through the troubled waters of launching a new concept. Thanks to my maintenance man, for bringing me his attorney, who became the first guinea pig and disciple of these concepts. I am indebted to Stephanie Brown Stearns for helping me proof and type several drafts. She was a constant encouragement and literary guide. I must acknowledge the distributors in my downline, without whose help none of this material would have come to pass. I am indebted to the Emeralds, Diamonds, Crowns, and Crown Ambassadors who were brave enough to try a new concept when they had already built large organizations through the traditional concept. I owe a large debt of gratitude to Suzy Guthy, my first publisher, a brave lady who introduced my name and materials to the world of network marketing. Most of all, I would like to thank Scott and Chris, my boys, who always understood when Dad had another coffee shop meeting or another page to write.

# Introduction

Although this is a book about networking, most of it will be about my experience with the Amway Network Marketing program. This is where my success and experience in networking have been. But many of the principles will work on other networking programs. Use what you can and discard the rest. If what you are doing is working, stay with it. If it isn't, or if you've tried before and couldn't succeed in networking, you might want to try the concepts presented here.

I am not trying to sell you on Amway. I don't care what you think of Amway; that has no significance to me. This material is not endorsed by Amway. They just happen to be the company with whom I was (and am) associated as I developed these concepts on networking. Obviously I am high on that company, or I'd be doing something else, but I don't care whether you are or not. We say, "Don't let your billfold get emotional."

This material is offered independently of the Amway Corporation and has not been endorsed or approved by the Amway Corporation or any of its officers or employees or any other multilevel marketing company. Likewise, neither the Amway Corporation nor any of its distributors or board members is authorized to market these materials, or any version of them, without the express written consent of the author.

## Disclaimer

Since I don't know with which network marketing company you are associated, or thinking about becoming associated, it is important that you find out which piece of literature contains your company's disclaimers. With Amway Corporation, you must give each prospect with whom you share the opportunity a copy of the latest version of "The Amway Sales and Marketing Plan" brochure (SA-4400). This contains the official average incomes and all the disclaimers required by the F. T. C. You must also state the following at the beginning of your presentation: "The examples I will use are simply to show you how the Plan works. They are not intended to project or promise any actual earnings. I'm giving you a brochure which fully describes the Plan and contains average profits, earnings, and sales figures and percentages."

Be sure you do these things in order to protect yourself and the company from claims of earnings misrepresentation. In Amway, if you sign up an associate, several copies of the form are included in the Sales and Product kit. Remember, the product portion of the kit is optional for new associates. Complete details are included in the *Amway Business Reference Manual* (SA-3145).

No one can guarantee that the techniques and approaches suggested in this material will work for you. I hope, however, that the ideas presented here will assist you in developing a strong, profitable business.

## Greetings

*"Bonjour, mes amis. Je parle un peu français."*
That means, "Howdy, folks. I speak a little French."

Now that I have tipped my hat to academia, and since I am not a professional writer, it would help me if you just let me talk to you as though we were sitting at a coffee shop having a cup of coffee. Is that okay?

I was raised in the foothills of the Great Smokey Mountains. Mountain folk are a proud lot, and most people understand what they mean. Sometimes city dwellers have a difficult time with my drawl, and I drive 'em crazy in Paris. Well, let's jump right in and get started.

## Targeted Audience

This guide is designed for the man on the street. (Excuse me, ladies: "Woman on the street" didn't sound too cool.) It is for those curious about network marketing. In particular, the hope is that it will tantalize those who tried traditional networking and gave up, or those currently involved who are floundering for lack of direction or focus.

I've tried to stick to teaching concepts and stay clear of network jargon. However, when I use terms like *Silver, Ruby, Direct, Pearl, Emerald, Diamond, Crown,* and *Crown Ambassador* I am referring to certain levels of achievement in that order. These are Amway terms because that's what I know. If you become interested in network marketing, you'll learn the terms your company uses.

## The Overtones of My Background

As W. Somerset Maugham wrote in *The Razor's Edge:*

It is very difficult to know people. For men and women are not only themselves, they are also the region in which they

13

were born, the city apartment or the farm in which they learned to walk, the games they played as children, the old wives' tales they overheard, the food they ate, the schools they attended, the sports they followed, the poets they read, and the God they believed in. You can *know* them only if you *are* them.

My background was so strongly influenced by the church, music, and real estate that you will hear the overtones of those themes coming through as I narrate my experiences in networking. Had I been an engineer, I would talk with you about the slide rule or the fulcrum. Please accept my illustrations and anecdotes as they are intended, and not as preaching.

I did try preaching once. The pastor was going to be gone one Sunday morning, so he asked me to preach. I was preaching on Sampson, but I got so nervous, I called him Tarzan all the way through the sermon.

## On Your Honor

The first thing I've got to do is put you on your honor. If after reading this book, you and your distributors decide to adopt any of the concepts taught here, you must be careful in every detail not to cause an abuse in any of the four following areas. They may not be clear now, but they will be after you read the book.

Because the legal department at Amway is concerned about potential abuse, I am required and desire to make you aware of these. You'll help me, won't you?

1. *Care should be taken not to depersonalize the individual.* Even though your entire team may help you sponsor an individual, it is important to maintain the spirit of Amway in its care for each individual distributor.

2. *Under the Amway Sales and Marketing Plan, vertical sponsoring may result in a significant financial detriment as compared to horizontal sponsoring.* A full disclosure of this difference must be made perfectly clear to all your distributors and prospective distributors.

3. *In particular, if a person has three strong friends, three doctors or three children of age, etc., as prospects, encourage him to personally sponsor them.* Under the Amway Sales and Marketing Plan, vertical sponsoring may result in a significant financial detriment as compared to horizontal sponsoring. For a further discussion, see chapter 15.

4. *Not everyone will market two hundred dollars in merchandise each month.* Many of my distributors do not. No one has to. We have only *choose to*'s, no *have to*'s.

# Program
# Notes

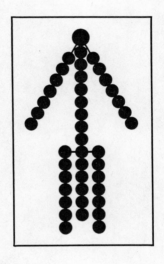

# One

# A Little of My Story

This is a little of my story. A few months ago I was in New York City for the Second Annual National Direct Distributors' Conference. Boy, did I feel like I was in tall cotton there, with so many Directs, Emeralds, Diamonds, Crowns, and Crown Ambassadors. Even the president of the company was there.

Some of us got together and had limousines pick up some of our new Directs at the airport and chauffeur them to the Waldorf-Astoria Hotel. Some of them were successful professionals, some were cowboys with boots and hats, and there was one hillbilly (I was the hillbilly). We had a banquet that was a seven-course meal; then we danced to the Peter Duchin Orchestra until they turned the lights out. We had a ball. Living the dream. What a life-style. Eating high off the hog.

## I Hid in the Outhouse and Ate the Scraps I Found in the School Yard

As I stood there in the Waldorf-Astoria, leaning over the balustrade taking pictures of the fun, I thought, *This is a long way from Frog Pond Holler*. I remembered that first Valentine card I gave to my first teacher. My mother had erased someone else's name and put my teacher's name on it. I remembered going to school in hand-me-down overalls with one of the galluses broken beyond repair and hanging down. My first piece of bubble gum was one I found on the school grounds—it had already been chewed. We usually went to school having had no breakfast, carrying no lunch, and expecting no supper when we returned. So I gathered scraps from the school yard and hid in the outhouse and ate them, until someone caught me doing it. I thought I was more hungry than ashamed; after that, I was more ashamed than hungry.

I remembered putting my things into a cardboard box and hitchhiking off to college. I wanted to study music because I felt God had called me to do that.

I have to tell you this one story. There I was in the department of music at a major school. I'd never had a music lesson to my name. I'd never had on a tie, much less a suit. I thought that dress-up for the President's Reception was khaki pants and a clean shirt.

Some of the older boys with far greater talent and musical experience than I decided to have some fun with me. They talked me into trying out for the university choir. Out of the entire university, the choir numbered twenty-six. They pumped me up about my ability to make it and took me over to where tryouts were being held. They knocked on the door and ran. I should have known something was up, but I just thought they were in a hurry.

When the lady whom I later discovered was the director of the choir opened the door, I noticed there was a group of choir officers sitting in there as well, to help with the tryouts.

They all seemed as shocked as I was. The director said, "Do you have an audition time?" I told her I didn't know what that meant. She explained and asked me, "What number are you going to do from your repertoire?" I told her that I didn't know what that meant, either. I just wanted to try out for the choir. She said, "What are you going to sing?"

I said, "I'll just sing a hymn, if that's all right."

She said, "All right."

I said, "Do you have a hymnbook?"

They scurried around and found one, and I picked out "Come Thou Almighty King." By now I'd figured out this was a pretty high-class group, and they wouldn't want to hear "I'll Fly Away."

She then asked, "Did you bring an accompanist?"

After she explained to me that meant someone to play the piano for me, I said, "Can't any of you play?" I wasn't trying to be funny.

Well, I sang it, putting in all the curlicues and special yodels on certain words, as I had heard Hank Williams do on the "Grand Ole Opry" on the radio at my uncle's house.

I noticed that some of my auditioners put their hands up by their mouths, and I could tell things weren't going well. I didn't know what was going wrong, but I have always been grateful to them for not laughing at me. When I finished, they clapped for me and were most gracious, but they didn't put me in the choir.

I flunked every course in the music department. But the teachers soon saw my commitment and began using their lunch hours and coffee breaks to get me caught up. Many nights I cried myself to sleep wondering if I would ever make it.

I made the choir the next year. They said that if I improved the next year as much as I did the first year, I'd be dangerous. I wound up with an earned doctorate in music theory and composition.

The boys who took me to try out apologized later for the prank.

I told them I hadn't gotten mad because I thought they were trying to help me.

This event helped me in life. Have you ever noticed that not everyone who pretends to be helping you—taking you to the door, knocking, and running—has your best interest at heart? It's not always easy to spot, is it? And when you realize, it makes you feel like a fool for being so vulnerable. Who was it who said, "When you seek revenge, you should first dig two graves"?

As you go through life, you can only hope that those who have the ultimate decisions in your "audition" will honor your sincere effort when the truth is finally made known to them.

Whoa. I'm getting ahead of myself. If I tell you everything now, you won't read the book. I tried to leave out that part you wouldn't read. If you'll just sort of remember where we are, I have some other things to tell you. I'll get back to the rest of the story at the Waldorf in the last chapter. Okay?

# Two

## What Is Network Marketing?

For the purposes of this book, the term *network marketing* refers only to that aspect of networking that relates to multilevel marketing. For a fuller definition of the term *networking* and all of its ramifications, see John Naisbitt's book *Megatrends*.

I understand that the Harvard School of Business now teaches network marketing. You will know what I mean by the term when I say it is the system used by many companies to market their products: Shaklee, Avon, Amway, Herbalife, Starcom, USA, Cambridge, Housewives Coupons, A. L. Williams Insurance Company, and so forth, all use some form of networking. Some of these are good companies, and some are already out of business. Anyway, Amway is the one that made the term famous. Therefore, I'll use my experience in Amway as the basis for this discussion.

The simplest explanation of networking goes like this: I sponsor you into my organization, you sponsor other people into yours, and they sponsor people into theirs. At some point, someone in the group reaches a certain level of production, breaks away from you, and starts dealing directly with the company instead of with you as his sponsor.

This is an oversimplification, but it will serve to identify what we mean by the term *network marketing*.

## Limitation of the Scope of This Guide

This is simply a book on how to build an organization in networking. It deals only with putting a team of people together, not with merchandising products. Obviously if you don't sell anything, you have no need for a team. See your company's literature for merchandising. Most companies have plenty of literature on merchandising and merchandise but none or very little on building an organization.

We teach that everyone strives to get ten customers and to do at least two hundred dollars worth of business per month. (Actually, their goal is one hundred P.V., but that is an in-house term that is explained once a person joins the network. One hundred P.V. often equals about two hundred dollars.) Not everyone in my organization does two hundred dollars worth of business per month. I wish they did. In fact, some of them don't do anything. But our goal is two hundred dollars in sales per distributor per month. It is not a free ride.

## The Ideal Is to Merchandise and Build Simultaneously

We seldom attain the ideal, but the best situation is to have a distributor begin merchandising and building simultaneously. However, some of them just won't do that. In the past, someone would sponsor a friend and then call him every night to see if he had sold anything to make the sponsor rich. Folks didn't like being bugged like that. They could see through it.

Obviously someone has to merchandise the products, but you don't have to open a store the day you break ground on a vacant lot. We let them grow into it, just like we let them grow into sponsoring distributors.

## Build a Portion of Your Structure First

It is my opinion that you should first build a portion of your organization and then have a training session on merchandising and encourage your distributors to switch over to your company's brands. The reason for building part of your team first is that you want to have a network or structure through which products can flow.

I assume you are familiar with your company's marketing plan. In Amway we use what is called the Amway Sales and Marketing Plan. We present that at every meeting and are required to give prospects and new distributors a copy of it to take home with them. That way we have covered all the bases. We do not change any item in it.

## Why Build a Portion of the Team First?

If Sears were going to put up a new store on a busy freeway, they wouldn't just pile all the products out on the side of the road and hire you to flag down the cars as they went by. This is pretty much the way networking has been in the past. Sears wouldn't do it that way. They would choose a place and build a structure; then they'd hire the personnel; last would come the merchandise and customers.

Thus, the two basic aspects of networking are: recruiting (building a team) and merchandising.

This manual deals only with the first of these aspects. If I were a physician writing a book on surgery, I wouldn't discuss how to market medicine from a pharmacy. Again, *no one can guarantee that the techniques and approaches suggested in this material will work for you. I hope, however, that the ideas presented here will assist you in developing a strong and profitable business.*

## When the Tide Comes In, All Ships Rise

Many companies are doing very well in networking. It is a good alternative to building all those shopping centers. All ships do rise when the tide comes in, and since we all fish out of the same pond, let's be fair and ethical with one another. Psychiatrists tell us it doesn't make us look any better to run someone else down. The antitrust laws deal with treating our competitors fairly. The better you look, the better we all look.

We shouldn't be like that church back in Tennessee. At their annual association meeting, the pastor of the First Baptist Church of Opossum Trot got up and gave his annual report: "We didn't have any additions this past year, but, thank the Lord, neither did the Methodists." If we can't help each other, let's try not to hurt each other.

The competition in networking is fierce because the stakes are so high. But if you start criticizing or lying about a competitor or subordinate, word gets around and you become less effective. You are like a bird with a wounded pinion; he never flies as high again.

The networking business is a very forgiving business, but it demands our highest and noblest effort because there is so much opportunity for abuse. Well, that's my sermon on networking.

# Three

## Why Did You Write This Book? A Need Gone Begging

I've been around network marketing now for a little over three years. Hardly a day goes by that I don't show the plan at least eight or ten times. I've looked at many other companies' deals. Most of them smother you with information about their company, their product, the potential income of their plans, but offer little or no practical, streetwise techniques on how to build the business. This is a need that has gone begging. Dreams and goals are great, but dreams and goals alone won't cut it.

No magnum opus here—more like the steps to Parnassus. This book is intended to be a practical guide from someone who has already built a fairly successful network marketing organization and is continuing to build. Mine's not the biggest organization around and not the smallest (Emerald Direct Distributor).

Those of us in network marketing have been inundated with information but starved to death for knowledge.

I look at good people whose hearts have been broken when they went out and made fools of themselves because they hadn't been given specific guidelines. Maybe they went to the family reunion, cornered all their relatives, and tried to sponsor them. Now they aren't even welcome back next year. This guide doesn't cover everything; it is designed to give you enough basic information to make you fairly knowledgeable on the subject of network marketing.

## Whiffenpoof Land

When I first got into networking, I worked like a Trojan but kept spinning my wheels. People would say, "Listen to tapes." I did. The tapes would say, "Dream." I dreamed. Then they would say, "Go to rallies." I'd go to rallies, and they'd say, "You've got to be committed, really want it, listen to tapes and read books." After about a year of this, I began to feel they and I *both* needed to be *committed*.

When I was a youngster, on Sundays I would go to the Baptist Church in the morning, to the Presbyterian in the afternoon, and to the Church of God in the evening. No, it wasn't because I was so spiritual; church was the center of my social life. That's where the girls were, and you didn't have to pay to get in. I never did learn to speak in tongues, but I have studied four other languages (just in case you need that to get into heaven).

Back in Cleveland, Tennessee, where I'm from, we would go to revival meetings. Sometimes people would get so excited that they would run up and down the aisle shouting and jumping benches. When they slowed down, they would ask, "Have you got it yet, brother?" Now, I'm not making fun because I went back every night, trying to "get it." And that's how I felt about much of the networking business, too. Most people were trying to find that "it" that makes it happen. It all seemed to be out there in never-never land.

What I ultimately found out about those who made it in the

company with which I am involved was: They had worked very hard and fast for a period; they had gotten a little bit lucky; they had built most of their business over many years; and they had been consistent, doing at least a little bit every day.

## Another Mousetrap

My original intention was to prepare written materials for my own organization, but the word got out and the world not only beat a path to my doorstep, but almost tore my door down. Some of them called it "a better mousetrap." I choose to call it *another* mousetrap. Use what you can of it. If there's some aspect of it you don't like, at least it will give you a point of departure. We now have something written down.

Since I am more of a teacher than a salesman, I like to work from document rather than from thought. It takes me a while to understand something, but when I do, I can reduce it to its simplest terms and get it into a form that is easy to understand. I am an average salesman, but I am a heck of a teacher.

When we hear something spoken, it appeals to our emotions. When we read it, it appeals to our intellect. So I began to put things on paper and analyze them. It was like working a crossword puzzle with some of the pieces missing. Later I began to find some of the missing pieces, and this guide is a result of that effort.

# Four

## End of Denial

When Team Sponsoring and the Seven-Deep Concept was first published in June 1985 under the title *Surrogate, Substitute Sponsoring and Structure,* it sent shock waves throughout the Amway world. It divided Amway distributorships right down the middle, just like Democrats and Republicans. Now, after two years, many of the major distributorships are using the concept in some form or another, although there are still a few pockets of die-hards. Most knowing people would agree that we are nearing the end of the denial.

The Amway Corporation was concerned, and I can certainly understand their concern. There I was, merely a Ruby Direct Distributor, new in the business, living in a small west Texas town, telling a highly successful, twenty-six-year-old, billion-dollar corporation how to build a business.

The corporation had seen many phony deals and systems come along before, and it immediately tossed this one into that category.

### Concern About Potential Abuse

Amway was already in the throes of a merchandising revolution, with new products and services such as M.C.I. The Team

Sponsoring and Seven-Deep Concept hit at about the same time, and there was an explosion of new sponsoring and merchandising. No human being could have predicted it. The company looked at my innovations with a jaundiced eye.

I continued to build my own business to the Emerald Direct Distributor level and am still building. They began to see that I was not going to bilk their distributors with my materials or try to exploit my opportunity. However, in the beginning, they probably thought I would.

We have taught at every instance to guard against depersonalization of the distributor and to explain the financial trade-off for security in the business when explaining the impact of vertical versus horizontal sponsoring. While there is opportunity for some to abuse the contemporary concept, there is probably no more than in the traditional concept. One can abuse anything. Some abuse the church, synagogue, or temple, and some abuse their families, whom they love. People even abuse their bodies by eating too much or by not exercising.

## A Chigger in a Bear Fight

Well, here we are two years later. After many phone calls, letters, tears, lost sleep, kicking, and hollering—mostly on my part as I tried to get my concepts approved—I began to feel like a chigger in a bear fight. About all that happened was the chigger caused the bear to have an uncomfortable itch. And the bear got a lot of honey out of the deal. But the chigger never stopped loving the bear.

Amway endorses no one's literature, but this presentation has been reviewed by their legal staff. I hasten to say they do not endorse or approve the concepts taught here, and neither they nor I can guarantee you success if you use this method. But for the tens of thousands of you good people who tried network marketing and couldn't make it work the traditional way, this may be an alternative for you. No guarantees, however.

I think Amway decided the potential benefits outweighed the potential abuses. They decided not to throw the baby out with the bath water. Now the distributors don't have to bootleg these concepts anymore.

There is only one Eiffel Tower and one *Mona Lisa,* and this is the only authorized version of Team Sponsoring and the Seven-Deep Concept. People ask me, "Is it all right if I just print up my own version of Team Sponsoring and the Seven-Deep Concept?"

I say, "No. This material is copyrighted." Can you imagine Irving Berlin's attorneys permitting a prostituted version of "White Christmas"?

# Five

## Integrity Mixed With New Blood

The secret, seldom-spoken fear that lurks within the deep recesses of the hearts and minds of all of us in networking, even in established companies, is, "What happens when the founder of the company dies or retires?" The cofounders of Amway are addressing this issue with the same sense of detail and care for their distributors and their distributors' customers as they have every problem since the business's inception.

The Amway Corporation gives everyone a chance to prove himself and his ideas. They have the highest integrity. This stems from its cofounders, Mr. Rich DeVos, President, and Mr. Jay Van Andel, Chairman of the Board. They are two real American heroes to many, myself included. They are very protective of their turf, and frankly, that is one of the reasons they have survived as the major leaders of network marketing.

Mr. DeVos and Mr. Van Andel have turned the day-to-day operations over to two new men with very impressive credentials: Mr. Bill Nicholson, Chief Operating Officer, and Mr. Otto Stolz, Chief Legal Counsel and Executive Vice-President–Administration. Some people call them Dr. Doom and Dr. Doom, but they're as smart as circus dogs. They have really shaken up the corporation in terms of getting rid of the fat, featherbedding, and corporate incest at the top, and in terms of developing new markets and services. The company is now lean and mean.

It appears to me that they have awakened a sleeping giant, given him a cup of coffee, a pat on the back, a kick in the rump, and a whole world of opportunities that none of us would ever have dreamed of.

They are two of the best things that have ever happened to Amway. They are also helping to groom the Van Andel and DeVos children for their destiny with the corporation. Nan Van Andel and Dick DeVos are already in powerful positions of leadership. They are bright, they are trusted, and they are and have been in intensive on-the-job training. They stand ready to take the helm.

# Overture

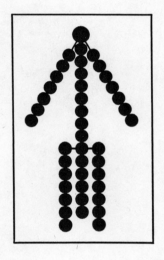

# Six

## Traditional Concepts

First of all, I have to give you a little of my history in networking. I got tricked into going over to someone's house after church one night. I asked what the meeting was for, and they said, "You'll like it." Since I was on the staff, I thought it must be a surprise party for the staff.

After we ate, they started drawing circles and stirring soap. I felt I had been tricked. Have you ever had that happen to you? After about three and a half hours, they wrestled me to the ground, and I saw the only way I was going to get out of there was to sign up. I gave them the hundred bucks and went home.

When I told one of my real estate partners that I knew how we could get rich, he said, "How?"

I said, "Selling Amway."

He said, "Selling soap?" He laughed at me so loudly that I went out back and threw my Amway kit over the fence into the dumpster. (I kept the products, because I loved them.)

I thought, *If my partner laughed at me, what would my students at the university do?* I had an image problem. I know that is simply a false impression of yourself, but I had it and I admit it. Can you identify with that?

## How I Got Sponsored for Real

A few years later, I was in a real estate project with another real estate partner—a major stockholder in a bank. He has an airplane and a fourteen-car garage. I also noticed that when we went anywhere, he never took any money with him, because he already had some there. I didn't know how he made his money. I'd seen that six-carat diamond his wife wore and another ring that is a miniature bale of diamonds. I knew he hadn't made that kind of money as an architect.

I found out he had this part-time business that was doing well, so I got him to tell me about it on April 15, 1983. He showed me I could market big-ticket items and not just sell soap. I no longer had an image problem. I knew I could now sponsor physicians, attorneys, bankers, students, farmers, and teachers, because there would be no image problem.

I asked his wife and him, "What does it take to go to the top?"

They said, "Twenty-five people [it's now twenty] each at the seventy-five hundred P.V. level for six months. That's called a Crown Ambassador, and it pays rather well."

I said, "You're kidding!"

Then I said, "Let's load my car up with kits." A 380SL will hold twelve kits. They left for the Caribbean for two weeks. When I got in my car, I wrote down in the front of my calendar that I was going to build this business, no matter what. I didn't care who wanted it and who didn't. I saw the big picture instantly.

I decided to get thirty distributors, just in case five quit. I started sponsoring like crazy. The first person I showed the plan to stole my kit. He said, "I'll pay you Friday," and I never saw him again.

One of the next ones gave me a hot check for five kits. That didn't even faze me. I sold those twelve kits and started taking checks and orders on the rest. However, I immediately saw that there was a dead cat on the line.

When my sponsors got back from their vacation, I was waiting for them. (Many of the people who have succeeded in the business say, "We try to take one week a month off and go somewhere to play." My sponsors *come home* one week a month. They built it right, didn't they?)

I said, "I must be doing something wrong."

They said, "Can't you sponsor anyone?"

I said, "Yes. I'm sponsoring everyone, but they aren't doing anything. In fact, most of them have already quit." Has that ever happened to you?

They sat me down and taught me the basic concepts of the traditional network marketing business. To this day, I've not met anyone who has a better grasp of it or a better ability to communicate that knowledge. They wean you really early, too.

## How the Traditional Plan Works
## (or Didn't Work for Me)

I can tell you in one sentence what those first people who tricked me took three and a half hours to explain. It's not good grammar, but it's good memory. If you can say, "Me-you-6-4-2," you've got it. That means that if I sponsor you, and you sponsor six, and each of those sponsors four, and each of those sponsors two, you have an organization with seventy-nine people in it. It would look like this:

That is the essence of the traditional plan. Some people got rich using it. Some still do. I didn't. It was blood and guts and the survival of the fittest. Most of the successful ones will tell you that. (If that system is working for you, hang in there. Don't change a thing. May your tribe increase.)

I began sponsoring and merchandising like crazy. I was working at it sixty to eighty hours a week, and my first bonus check was for $36. I made Silver, which is the first month of Direct Distributor qualification, in eleven months. (In Amway, Silver means your organization does at least seventy-five hundred P.V., or about $15,000 in business volume. When you qualify as a Silver for three months in succession, you break away from your sponsor and deal directly with the company. Your sponsor, if qualified, receives a 3 percent override.)

But I am embarrassed to tell you that after I made Direct, I couldn't hold it. And I'm at least average. I knew that my friends didn't have very good odds at ever making it, since they couldn't spend sixty hours a week on it because of their professions. I said to myself, *That dog won't hunt*. I saw this thing was too good and too close to being great, but it was breaking too many people this way.

I am envious of those who were able to build large networks and get rich using the traditional concepts. You know why?

Because they were able to do something I couldn't. But since there are more of us who couldn't make it work than there are of those, at least we deserve a shot at the alternative. When I got into the business, my sponsor said, "Fail my way first." So I did. Maybe you did, too. Now let's have a shot at the other way.

## Areas I Couldn't Get a Handle On

Even though I failed, I didn't quit. I drove everybody crazy asking them questions. When I got back to my house, I'd write down the answers. I began to notice that some of my friends were as confused as I was in some areas:

1. Fear of failure ("Yeah, but could I do it?")
2. Would all those people in that plan do their two hundred dollars per month?*
3. Momentum (How to get enough people going at the same time in order to round up seventy-five hundred P.V.)

But the three that killed me were:

4. I couldn't find a place to focus.
5. People quit faster than I could sponsor them.
6. I had made competitors of six of my best friends.

Have any of those areas ever concerned you? Let's go a little further with some of these.

## The Mud Plan

I couldn't find a place to focus in the traditional plan. It used to be affectionately called the "Mud Plan." You threw some

* Adherence to the method described herein does not guarantee or promise that all of your people will do their two hundred dollars per month. Not everyone in my group does two hundred dollars per month.

mud up against a wall and hoped some of it stuck. I began to ask myself, "What is wrong with it?" and "How do we correct it?"

## People Quit Faster Than I Could Sponsor Them

The first thing that screamed out at me was that people quit faster than I could sponsor them. It was like a sieve. They fell out the bottom faster than I could put them in the top. Do you know what I'm talking about?

## I Had Made Competitors Out of Six of My Best Friends

Another serious problem was that I went out and sponsored six of my best friends and found I had made competitors out of them. Is your phone ringing? Let me show you.

I go out and sponsor six friends. Now Joe and Bill both know Don. Joe doesn't want Bill over at his house while he's talking to Don, because Bill wants Don in his group. They've become competitors, and they'll never be in the same group. One might just as well be Sears and the other Montgomery Ward.

It wasn't as though I had hit a brick wall; it was more like trying to lasso an amoeba. I decided I was going to have to find a solution to some of these problems, or else I was going to have to get out. I couldn't keep dragging my family and friends from tape to tape, book to book, and rally to rally.

The answer is so simple that wise men stumble over it. That shouldn't surprise any of us, though, should it? The Bible says that "God hath chosen the foolish things of the world to confound the wise. . ." (1 Corinthians 1:27).

Let's have a shot at the other way.

# Exposition

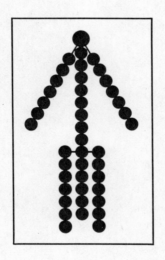

# Seven

## Avant-Garde (Contemporary) Concepts

The first question I asked myself was, "What if we could remove the competition and put folks on the same team?"

If you see this, you won't sleep tonight. It is as simple as the yo-yo. I don't know why no one thought of it in twenty-six years, but they didn't. If you don't see it, we say just go home and forget it and watch TV. We call TV the Electric Income Reducer.

### Build Three Teams Seven-Deep, One at a Time

Here it is. Let's say you sponsor Joe:

Now let's say you and Joe both know Don. Instead of putting Don in as a competitor to Joe, we put him under Joe, so of everything Don does, Joe and you both get a little. You see, you trade a little of your cut for the security. It looks like this:

Joe then says, "If that's the way it works, I'll put my son's tennis coach in there under Don."

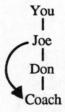

Don says, "I'll put my pastor in there."

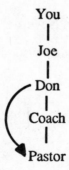

The coach says, "I know this petroleum engineer in Midland who is driving a taxi now. I'll put him under the pastor."

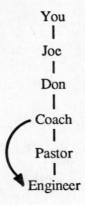

The pastor says, "I don't know a soul, and all I want to do is buy wholesale." Joe sponsors his dentist:

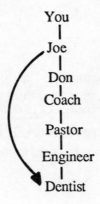

The dentist sponsors his son, who is a university student.

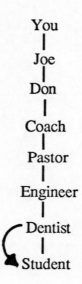

As soon as you get a team seven-deep, you start building your second team seven-deep, then your third team seven-deep. We'll explain why seven-deep a little later.

Do you see the difference between the traditional and the contemporary? Look at them in the two figures on the next page.

**Traditional Way:**
Me – You – 6 – 4 – 2

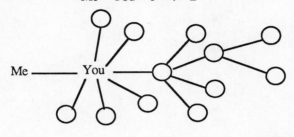

**Seven – Deep:**

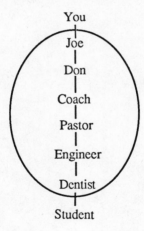

You
|
Joe
|
Don
|
Coach
|
Pastor
|
Engineer
|
Dentist
|
Student

Notice that in the traditional way, there is one person looking for six. In the new, there are six looking for one. Do you see how much more powerful that is?

The old looks like a wagon wheel and goes about as fast. The new Seven-Deep Concept is like a jet stream, and it just goes *zoooom*.

After you have built your first team seven-deep, build your

second team the same way. Do not start team two until you have finished team one. It should look something like this:

You

```
    1       1
    2       2
    3       3
    4       4
    5       5
    6       6
    7       7
```

Now build your third team the same way. Do not start it until your second team, or leg, is seven-deep.

You

```
    1     1     1
    2     2     2
    3     3     3
    4     4     4
    5     5     5
    6     6     6
    7     7     7
```

## You Are In Control

Team Sponsoring and the Seven-Deep Concept put you in control. No longer are you dependent on any single distributor. No one can stop you. It unlocks the multilevel marketing system. Let's look at the traditional way.

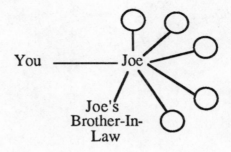

You have sponsored Joe, and he has sponsored his brother-in-law as one of his six. You offer to help and he says, "No. He's sensitive. I'd better just handle him myself. You know, he's my wife's brother, and they're a little funny."

You're dead. You can't go any further. All you can do is help him find someone with whom he'll let you work.

Let's assume you have the same situation with Team Sponsoring. You have built two legs seven-deep and are at number four on leg three. This is Joe's brother-in-law, and Joe is number three, just above him. It looks like this:

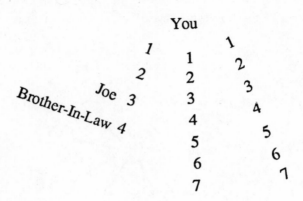

The brother-in-law, for whatever reason, won't give you a name. Maybe Joe doesn't want you to talk to him; maybe the brother-in-law has already gotten his friends and relatives into other deals that didn't work and the fear of failure has him in its grasp. Here's how we solve that problem. The Amway Corporation uses "foster sponsoring" in its international business. However, in the past, distributors did it with no structure in mind on a hit-or-miss basis.

The way we use it is this: When we can't get a name out of number three or number four, we go over them, to number two. He may say, "I know this doctor who would like to get into the business. Tell number four that if he'll go ahead and get his mother, brother, and pastor, I'll put the doctor under them."

Leg three now looks like this:

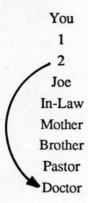

You
1
2
Joe
In-Law
Mother
Brother
Pastor
Doctor

What have we done? We've primed the pump. You city folk may not know what that means, but out in west Texas and in Tennessee, they know. What you've done is removed the fear of failure from Joe's brother-in-law.

Now watch this. If he doesn't put his mother, brother, and pastor in, we put the doctor under him anyway, because we don't get paid until he does. The fact that he might make a little doesn't hurt us. It would then look like this:

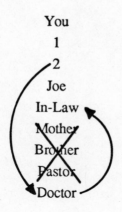

You
1
2
Joe
In-Law
Mother
Brother
Pastor
Doctor

## Summary

That brings you up to date on Team Sponsoring and the Seven-Deep Concept, Structure, and Foster (Surrogate) Sponsoring, which unlocks the network marketing system. Next I'm going to discuss some of the nuances that have evolved since we first started the concept in January 1985 and the questions I am asked most often.

# Development

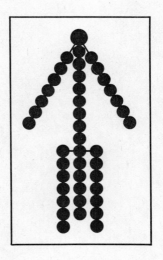

# **Eight**

## The Twenty Most Often Asked Questions

We started using Team Sponsoring and the Seven-Deep Concept (sometimes we just call it "Seven-Deep") in January 1985. Our first writing on it was published in June 1985. If you have been around the world of networking, you have some idea of the impact it has had on that business, especially on Amway. I am told that practically every major pin (leader) and almost every country in which they operate uses it. In fact, I do not know of a country that doesn't.

It's like that song from World War I (long before my time) that asks, "How ya gonna keep 'em down on the farm, after they've seen Paree?" Once they've seen the new concepts, they seldom go back to the traditional.

### Twenty Questions

1. *What changes have you made since you first came out with Team Sponsoring and the Seven-Deep Concept?*

Basically, we have kept the concept intact but have refined and streamlined it. We still teach people to get three legs seven-deep and not to start the second leg until they have finished the first, and the same for the third leg. The main exception is if a distributor has three sons, three brothers, three doctors, and so forth. He might want to put them in three different legs. Be careful with this, though. I would encourage a person in this situation to wait to sponsor the other two until I saw that he was going to build the business. I know I am going to be helping him build leg one, but if he isn't working, I am not going to be helping in legs two and three, and they would probably sit out there and die. Can you see that?

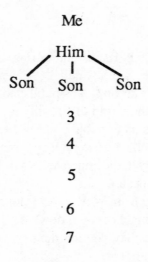

You see, I am going on to seven-deep, whether he goes on or not. Then I'm going to build my second and third legs. But I'm surely not going to build his other two legs if he's not working. If he's not working, then I would encourage him to put the other two downline in the long leg, so I could afford to work with them. It would then look like this:

Me

Him

Son

3

4

5

6

7

Son

Son

Why did I put them as numbers eight and nine, and not numbers three and four? Well, you see, I was probably already to number seven before I realized he wasn't going to do anything. Why wouldn't I start my second leg with them? That I am sure is obvious to you: They are his prospects, and if I put them in my other leg, they wouldn't be in his group. In the following cases, you might encourage a distributor to start legs four, five, and six a little sooner than previously recommended: an unusually strong person, or a relatively new person who has decided to go full-time. This way he could possibly increase his profitability earlier and the legs could be incubating while he continues to build his first three legs.

2. *If you build three teams seven-deep, don't you just have twenty-one distributors, whereas in the traditional "me-you-6-4-2," you have seventy-nine? Don't these twenty-one have to merchandise a lot more products?*

Well, this is something we didn't address in our last writing. It was obvious to us because we were already doing it.

I'm going to answer this at the same time I answer question

four. That way, I'll only have to do one illustration. Is that okay? We won't tell everyone, but we'll tell you.

3. *Suppose I built three teams seven-deep and the first leg died before I got back to it?*

This is more usual than unusual. If you are not building quickly, your people will become frustrated and quit on you. Can you imagine how frustrated people became when they were trying to build six teams at once?

There is also a little bit of envy going on here. You see, you've been working in leg one, and you have a leader about ready to go to work. He feels very comfortable while you are doing the presentations with him. You begin to ease him into going solo.

Now when you go over to build leg two, you are weaning him. But he feels abandoned because he can't do it as well as you could. Sometimes he'll pout. Sometimes he'll throw a temper tantrum. But you see, it doesn't matter. It's your time, and you can spend it anywhere you want to. Let him pout for a while. We're going to come back over and unruffle his tail feathers in a minute.

This also happens when you wean a Direct Distributor. He'll holler and tell everyone that you've abandoned him and are spending all your time helping that cowboy from Fort Worth, even when the Direct from Fort Worth is downline from him. He'd rather you helped him go Pearl.

4. *I have built three legs seven-deep and it appears that I am the only one having any success. What can I do?*

Well, let's look at it. You have your three teams built. If anyone is having any success, who is it? I can't use the term "making any money" because of the disclaimers involved in income representations. Just see your company's bonus structure for income figures.

Me

You

```
  1       1         1
    2     2           2
      3   3             3
        4 4 ◀— Pouting  4
      5   5               5
    6     6             6
  7       7         7
```

Obviously it is you, because all the distributors are in your group. Now watch what happens. Let's say that I have sponsored you and you are the one trying to go Direct. You have your three legs seven-deep. Number four in leg one is the one pouting. You go over to him and say, "Hey, number four, I've learned how to build this business. I have my three teams seven-deep. Now my sponsor and I are going to come over and help you build your three legs. Get out your calendar."

He runs home and tells his wife that this business is a piece of cake. He struts around like a flat-footed duck on a hot rock. "Joe [that's you] and his sponsor are going to help us build our three teams now, and I know we can do it because Joe's sponsor helped him build his three. With all three of us working, it'll go faster." Your team now looks like this:

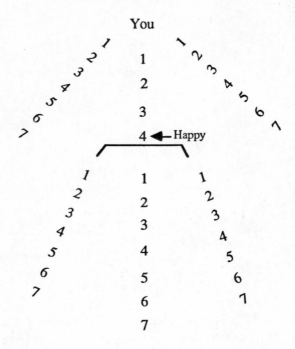

You have now cloned yourself. Number four has twenty-one in his group, and they're all in yours, too.

By now word has spread over to legs two and three. Somebody over there is just waiting to see if he is to be the one tapped on the shoulder. Let's say that in leg two it is number five and her husband. They get three legs seven-deep. They now have twenty-one in their group. Then the doctor and his wife, number seven in leg two, get their three teams seven-deep. They now also have twenty-one in their group.

I believe that if you count, you will see that you now have over seventy-nine people in your three teams. (Now we have answered question two.) But rather than having them in competition with

66

one another, you have them on three teams. It would look like this:

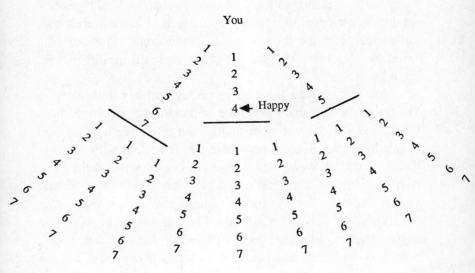

Do you see that you have now gone to the second power, so to speak? If you took it to the third power—that is, if you helped those at the bottom of the legs do the same thing—you could be headed for your next pin or award level. We are assuming that your organization is merchandising a sufficient amount of products. I don't know of anyone's organization where *all* the distributors are merchandising. In my organization they certainly aren't. But some of them will, if you or your company have trained them.

5. *I have a leg thirty-deep and no one is moving any products. What now?*

My question to you is: How many products did they move before they got in? I'm merely teaching you how to build a team;

you still have to train them and teach them how to merchandise the products. As soon as you recruit them, take them to your company's workshop to learn how to merchandise and to receive product knowledge. Our follow-up meeting is at the warehouse, where they can see the products. If you don't work out of a warehouse or center, you still get your products from somewhere. Take them there.

If you tell me you have only one leg and it's thirty-deep, I know you haven't understood the importance of structure. First of all, you should have them divided out into three legs, instead of one long one. But you may have two other legs with seven in them and still have one with thirty in it. Let's say that is the case.

If you were building right, you probably wouldn't know that your leg is thirty-deep. Why not? Because if you are sponsoring equals and up, one out of seven is likely to build his own three teams. That means that seven goes into thirty at least four times, with four opportunities to build three teams seven-deep. Let me illustrate it for you:

# The Twenty Most Often Asked Questions

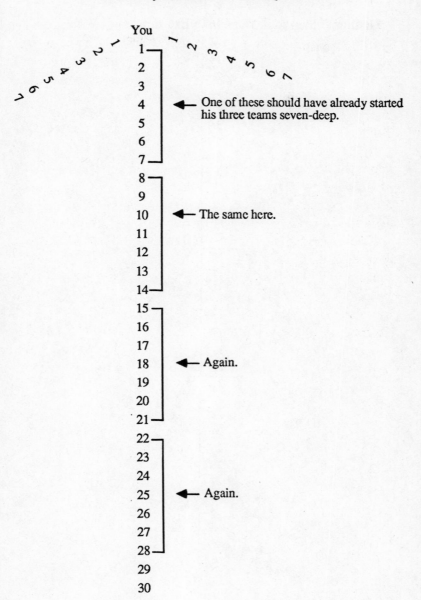

You

1
2
3
4 ← One of these should have already started his three teams seven-deep.
5
6
7

8
9
10 ← The same here.
11
12
13
14

15
16
17
18 ← Again.
19
20
21

22
23
24
25 ← Again.
26
27
28
29
30

It should then look something like this:

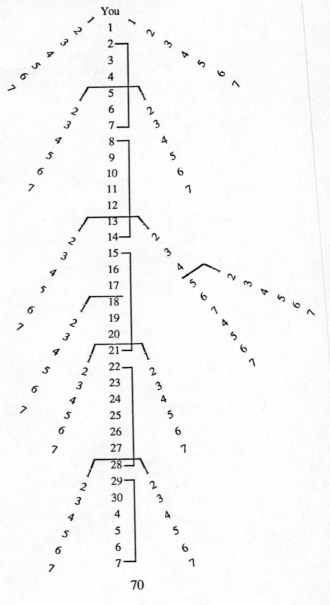

Is it obvious which one of the legs is the trunk leg? Is it obvious where you should be working? Is it obvious why you don't want to get lost out on one of their second or third legs?

If you are doing it right, one of these would probably already have broken off from you and become a Direct Distributor dealing directly with the company. You would then no longer know how deep the leg went, because the company would send the records to your new Direct Distributor. You understand, of course, that if you met all the other qualifications required of your company, you would probably get an override. This is not true of all multilevel marketing companies, but the Amway Corporation does pay an override, if you meet the qualifications. See the manual of your company for percentages.

6. *What is the coffee shop blitz, and how does it work?*

That question doesn't fall into the scope of this book. But because I am asked it so often, I wanted to tell you that we will cover it in the next book.

7. *Do you still teach your people to start their second and third legs even though they might not have a leader in a particular leg yet?*

Yes. The first thing we need to do is make you a leader. When you have built three teams, you will have gotten most of the skinned knees and bloody noses you are going to get from this business. You'll be a leader. Then you clone yourself.

If you are sponsoring equals and up, you have leaders. You just haven't taught them how to lead. You don't find leaders, you develop them. Oh, every now and then, you'll get a "gimmey." But if you are going to be big in this business, you must learn to develop leaders.

8. *How do you define a leader?*

A leader is someone who has built three teams seven-deep, or who will make a sufficient commitment to the business to let me teach him to build three teams seven-deep.

9. *I have four pages of prospects. Where do you suggest I start?*

10. *I can sponsor anyone. I've put twenty-five into my group, but no one else is sponsoring. What should I do?*

These are really the same problem. Both of these people are "hosses." They are the type you look for. However, sometimes their greatest strength—sponsoring—becomes their downfall.

I think the worst thing you can have in this business is a long prospect list. When I said that recently at the National Direct Distributors' Meeting in New York at the Waldorf-Astoria Hotel, the whole group gasped. See if you don't agree with me. Watch this scenario.

You have built three teams seven-deep, but *you* have put all the people in. Can you see that there is no glue to hold the teams together? No one but you has made a commitment to sponsoring or building. Now suppose you can get an ole boy to put his mother in under him. Wow! Is he committed! He's married to that group. Suppose he puts his son in there. He'd die to build that leg. But if they are all *your* prospects, it's also all *your* team, and they don't care. That means you are playing pitcher, coach, first base, batter, fielder, and shortstop. It's hard to win a game like that.

That's why one of my Crown Direct friends says, "As soon as you get a leg seven-deep, you get them all together for a potluck supper." You want to find out who can hit a single and who can knock a home run. You want to find out who can steal bases, who can catch the ball, and who has the best equipment or tools. You want to find out who'll bring the Kool-Aid, who'll bring the cookies, and who can just hug people and help develop the right *esprit de corps*. You know—who can sponsor, who can merchandise, and who can make people feel good.

**11.** *Where do you put your prospects when you are working with someone who is building three legs seven-deep?*

I go with the longest and strongest suit, just as in bridge. I don't always know which of the three legs is going to be the strongest, but usually it is leg one. If I don't have a Direct in that leg, I'm going to keep teaching people in that one leg to get three legs seven-deep. But I stay in the trunk, or deepest leg, which I don't trust to anyone but me. If everyone in there quits, I still know there is going to be a Direct in that leg, because I am going to build it. I can't get out of it until I get a Direct, and even then, not completely.

**12.** *When do you get out of a leg?*

I don't know. I never have yet. That's a little facetious, but basically, I don't leave it until I get it to Profit-Sharing, because my job isn't finished until then. I think it's important to have Directs backed up by Directs. The company I am in pays you the best when your legs are Profit-Sharing Directs. See your own manual.

**13.** *Isn't there more potential profit in "me-you-6-4-2" than in three legs seven-deep?*

Potentially, yes. We still teach you to build six legs. We just say build them three at a time. We feel that it is better to trade some of your cut for the security.

*Under the Amway Sales and Marketing Plan, vertical sponsoring may result in a significant financial detriment as compared to horizontal sponsoring.*

14. *When do I start legs four, five, and six?*

We teach our people to start leg four when they get one qualified—that is, to Silver. When you get two legs qualified, start leg five, and so on.

15. *What do you think of automatic renewals?*

This is an in-house question, but I do have an opinion on it. It's great for Directs. But if there are eight or ten sharp distributors between me and a Direct, there is little incentive for me to work with them. If one doesn't renew, I can sponsor him in a leg where I am working and perhaps he will be the new Direct.

16. *How do you sponsor distributors who used to be in networking and quit?*

We call them *retreads.* I just say to them, "Now that it is so easy to build, wouldn't it be a shame for you not to harvest all that experience?"

Many people who are getting in now are people who tried before and, for some reason or another, got out. There are many sharp people out there who will take another look at this with you. Did you know that there are a number of people out there who used to be vice-presidents, managers, cofounders, Directs, Rubies, Pearls, and up who got tired and quit, trying to build the traditional way?

With my company, they have to have been inactive for at least six months before joining another organization. If there is any doubt, stay away from them. It is important not to proselyte distributors from other groups. It is a violation of most companies' codes of ethics. When in doubt, don't.

But since we all fish out of the same barrel, be sure. A simple letter of inquiry to corporate headquarters as to the status of a former distributor may save you a lot of headaches. I have a wonderful young man in my organization who lost an entire Silver Producer leg because he was confused about that point. Fortunately for me, but not for him, the person he lost the leg to was a Direct Distributor in my organization between him and me. That'll knock you to your knees. It didn't keep him down for long; he is in Diamond qualification now.

Do you know what people are saying to us now and will be saying in the future? It's not, "I tried that and it didn't work." I believe it's going to be (and in some cases already is), "I got in and sponsored one person, he went Direct, and I forgot to renew."

17. *How do you supply products?*
The same as we did before.

18. *I want to go full-time but don't know what to do or where to go to work.*
Don't do it. At least in most cases, don't go full time. I remember going to my sponsor early in my multilevel marketing career and telling her of this fellow who had lost his job and wanted to go full time. I was elated. She said, "That scares me." I didn't know what she meant, but I do now. I suggest you use common sense and tell them to get a job to pay the bills with until they have this business sufficiently built.

However, there is a new breed of cat coming along. He has an independent income, or his profession is played out, or he is burnt out. Maybe he is independently wealthy and wants a new challenge. Also, with the products and services we now have, it is possible to go Direct with a small organization.

Isn't the hardest thing in this business finding enough people who will let you work with them? We have that down to a science, but it will take a little longer than the nature of this little manual. I promise to get it to you. It unlocks your calendar.

### 19. *Why the number seven?*

Nothing spectacular. We have just found over the years that whether it's banking, insurance, real estate, the fast-food field, or the church, you can usually count on only about one in seven to emulate what you do. Someone said, "You can't sponsor all good people. Likewise, you can't sponsor all bad people." We just play the odds.

Many people ask, "Is it because you only pay seven levels deep?" It has nothing to do with the depth to which it pays. The network company in which I am a distributor pays for any business that can ever be traced to you. Obviously, the closer it is to you, the bigger your cut.

If your company only pays three levels deep, the Seven-Deep Concept won't work for you. If it only pays five-deep, it won't work. However, perhaps there are other aspects of it that you could use.

If the company only paid seven-deep, it would be my luck that the eighth person would be the "hoss" that wanted to build a dynasty.

In fact, my sponsors told me that "about 80 percent of the people you get into your network won't do much except maybe buy wholesale, but that 20 percent could eventually make you wealthy." That's one in five. I just stretched the odds and said it's okay if we can get one in seven.

The worst any of my friends could do was to buy products

wholesale the rest of their lives. They couldn't be hurt since they could get their money back any time they wanted it.

The eighty-twenty statement didn't bother me. I knew that down at the church 80 percent of the people wouldn't tithe, sing in the choir, or teach Sunday school. I just figured I couldn't expect to do any better than Jesus.

20. *How does your volume using these new concepts compare with your volume using the traditional concepts?*

What you are saying is, "The proof is in the pudding," isn't it? Using the traditional methods, I couldn't even requalify as a Direct Distributor. I had made Direct, but I could never get back up there.

My first full year of using the new concepts, three of my legs, or teams, produced $566,874.34 in volume. To put that into perspective, that is more volume than the entire Amway Corporation did in its first year in business. Of course, you have to consider the inflation factor.

These concepts have worked for others, as well as for me. However, there is no guarantee they will work for you. At best, these concepts are an alternative. They are not touted as a "cure-all." If you don't work, these concepts won't work.

## The Potential Power of Combining Team Sponsoring and the Seven-Deep Concept

If you will look at the illustration on the next page, I'll try to show you very vividly the power of the combination of Team Sponsoring and the Seven-Deep Concept.

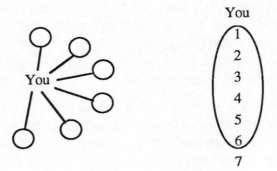

Do you see that the one on the left is the traditional method and is one person looking for six? On the right, there are six looking for one distributor. Do you see the difference?

If you'll let me play with your mind for just a minute, I want you to use your imagination a bit. I got this from some of my Directs who are cowboys. Have you ever been to a rodeo or seen one on TV? In the calf roping event, the cowboy sits on his horse in a box, with his rope in hand. They are about to turn the calf loose from a second box, and he is going to try to rope it on a dead run in a few seconds. When they pull the gate and the horse charges and the calf charges, the cowboy tries to rope the calf. Sometimes he ropes the calf, and sometimes he doesn't.

Now don't press me too hard on this illustration, but what if? What if you not only had the cowboy in the box ready to rope when the calf is turned loose, but you also had four cowboys standing still on the ground, ready to rope the calf? Also, what if a sixth cowboy were sitting beside the calf's box with a rope right in front of the calf's head?

It would be pretty hard to miss that calf under those conditions, wouldn't it? Well, play with that a little.

Turn it around now, and do it the old way. The cowboy is sitting there in the box on his horse and instead of one calf, they turn six calves loose and expect him to rope all six as effectively as all six of those previous cowboys had roped one calf. Is it becoming clearer to you?

If you are not the cowboy type, try this: Would it be easier for one person to locate six lost children in the woods or for six people to find one lost child?

# Recapitulation

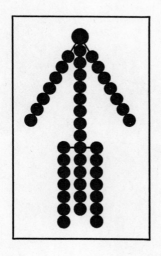

# Nine

## The Two-Minute Coffee Shop Presentation

In the two-minute presentation, all you are doing is giving your prospect the concept of your business. I will tell you the one I use for my business, and perhaps you can adapt it to your networking business.

> Doctor Jones, I'm going to tell you three things: what we market, how we market it, and what you would need to do if you decided to help us. At the end of each of these, I am going to ask you if you have understood me.
>
> We market many things, but I am only going to show you three of our products: M.C.I. [explain how it works]; ULTIMATE™ Travel Network [explain]; Mail-order catalog business [explain].
>
> Now, Doctor Jones, if you were sitting over there in that other booth talking with your cousin, you could explain that, couldn't you?
>
> Now I'm going to tell you the second thing, which is how we market our products, or how we put together a team of about seventy-five to a hundred people as a network.

Then I explain "me-you-6-4-2" to him, followed by the Team Sponsoring Seven-Deep Concept. Now I say again, "Doctor

Jones, couldn't you explain that to your cousin, if you were sitting over there in that booth with him?

"Third is what you'd need to know if you decide to help us build a business." Then I explain the ten steps, such as making a list of prospects, listening to tapes, getting a pocket (or purse) calendar, and so forth.

I close by saying, "Now, Doctor Jones, if you were going to help us, would you have any problems with any of those ten steps?" We usually talk about them, and then I say, "Well, let's get the paperwork out of the way."

If the plan is shown to him at lunch, I do this from the time the waitress takes the order until she brings the food. Then we sit there and talk about it as we eat. I don't care if he joins then or not. I tell him, "If it isn't as good in the morning as it was today, it wasn't much of a deal." But I do try to close, because I don't want to be just a storyteller.

# Ten

## Necessity Is the Mother of Invention

How did I arrive at the two-minute coffee shop presentation? Necessity is the mother of invention. It also came as a baby, not a full-grown idea. It came in two segments: the coffee shop presentation and the two-minute presentation.

### How the Coffee Shop Presentation Developed

I was a single parent, living in a small town and commuting to a large town to build my business. As a result, when I invited someone to look at the business, I couldn't take them all the way back to the other town. My sponsors were retired from the business and weren't holding meetings. I had no choice but to hold my meetings in the coffee shop. I always tipped well, so the owner and waitresses didn't mind. I thought that was the least I could do, since they paid the rent and the utility bills.

### How the Two-Minute Presentation Developed

One of the things that I remembered most about the time I was tricked into going to an Amway meeting was that it lasted three and a half hours. That left a bad taste in my mouth. (I know it wasn't Amway, but that was the only association I had with the company at the time.) I learned that I could compress the three basic concepts of the business within a two-minute overview.

From the time the waitress took our order until she returned with it, I could:

1. Tell them about three products—M.C.I., the ULTIMATE™ Travel Network, the catalog mail-order business, or any three I chose—but no more than three.

2. Tell them the concept of the business: "me-you-6-4-2" and Team Sponsoring and the Seven-Deep Concept.

3. Tell them what they would need to do if they were going to help me (the ten steps).

I then invited them over to one of my other distributors' homes for a full presentation of the business.

Instead of being able to do six meetings a week the traditional way (six nights a week), I could now do a coffee shop presentation with someone before he went to work in the morning, another at morning and afternoon coffee break time, and another after work on the way home. I also began taking three lunches (no, I didn't eat all of them). That left my evenings free if my boys and I wanted to go to church, the opera, or a ball game. We now lived like other human beings.

If I wanted to work in the evening with people who just couldn't meet during the day, I would schedule one at 6:00, one at 6:30, and one at 7:00, so I was headed for home by 7:30. I always had all three meetings at the same coffee shop, so they traveled and I didn't. That way, I didn't waste any time traveling.

By doing it this way, I discovered some serendipities:

1. The people I met with liked the coffee shop because it was neutral territory. They knew there wouldn't be a big group there.

Also, they could leave whenever they wanted. They didn't have to clean up the house, and they didn't have to be nice about your idea just because you had invited yourself into their home.

2. We learned that no longer did we have to have both husband and wife at the meeting. When it was a soap business, it was virtually impossible for the man to build the business without the wife. Now, with all the available products and services, either one or both can build very successfully. It's better if you have both, but you certainly don't have to have both.

3. Imagine this. I have just met you. I invite you to come and bring your wife to one of my distributors' homes, where there will be a "business opportunity" presented. What is going through your mind? First of all, we have just met; you haven't even told your wife that yet. You are supposed to go with me or meet me at a stranger's house. You're probably thinking, *Who is this guy, to be inviting me over to someone else's house?* And we wonder why we had no-shows. After you've joined, you'll be happy to meet me at anyone's house, whether you know them or not, but not at this stage.

4. This solved another knotty problem. Let me set the scene for you. Some hotshot comes to your house and sponsors you and your wife. He then gets you to "dreaming" and says, "Now you invite all your friends over to your house Thursday night, but don't tell them what they are coming to see. If you've got any credibility, you can get ten or fifteen. I'll come over and put the whammy on them."

In your new enthusiasm you tell him, "I can get fifty." He comes over to your home Thursday evening and meets with you and four of your best friends. They are sitting there in the living room, mad. After it's over, you may or may not get them. But those you don't get may never speak to you again because you tricked them.

## Are You Saying Don't Have Home Meetings?

No. Many people have built, and are still building, successful businesses using this type of meeting. In fact, some of my strongest Directs use the home meeting very effectively, and so do I. We just don't take chances with it. We stack the deck, so to speak, by sponsoring them, or exposing them to our business first at the coffee shop. The coffee shop meeting is just an alternative that complements the home meeting, not a replacement for it.

You see, by preselling or prequalifying them at the coffee shop meeting, we can remove some of the potential abuse that used to go on in tricking someone into coming to a home meeting. Even if we could find an individual to invite to a home meeting for a look at the business, one who had never been tricked before, how many do you think he could find who had never been to one?

If you talk to someone who was in the business and quit, or was tricked into a presentation at a home, he says, "I like that coffee shop idea. I never could pull that other stuff on my friends, and my wife didn't like it, either. She'll like this."

To summarize, we recruit the people at the coffee shop meetings and then invite them to the home meeting to meet one another and hear a full presentation. They think it's a "happening" then, rather than a "scalping."

## The Professional Approach

I still teach the professional approach. I don't just say, "Come and get in my Amway business." The mind is the laziest organ in the body; it will take the path of least resistance and make a decision on the information it has. The mind thinks, *It's a door-to-door soap company.*

I ask them, "Would you help me market M.C.I. and some other companies' products using that network marketing system Amway made famous?" That's honest and straightforward, but it has some nuance to it.

I tell folks up front the kind of products we are marketing and that "we use that network marketing system Amway made famous." That way, when they get to the coffee shop or the home, they aren't mad at you or Amway. They know it has to do with Amway.

How did I arrive at the idea for a coffee shop blitz? I had an orthodontist in my group who had Mondays off. We told his distributors that we would be at the coffee shop from 10:00 A.M. to 5:00 P.M. They could come and bring a prospect, as long as they came on the hour. This is also how the team concept developed.

From that very loose beginning, we developed it to the slick, well-oiled machine it is now, with every slot accounted for.

## How Did You Come Up With Team Sponsoring and the Seven-Deep Concept?

I've already told you how necessity required that some of the smaller ideas within the entire concept be developed. But when you consider the overall concept, God just gave it to me. Why me? I don't know. I can only guess. But I do have some strong hunches. You may call it inspiration or creativity, but I believe all those come from Him.

At the risk of being misunderstood, and not wanting to offend you, that is the only explanation for it that I can imagine. I wish I could tell you that it is because I am so much smarter than those who have been around network marketing for the past twenty-seven years, but you'd find out that wasn't true.

I get very careful and skeptical when someone comes at me with a real estate deal and starts getting religious. I grab for my billfold and hold on. I can only hope that you understand my intent and my feeling of obligation to share the idea.

First of all, it came as a baby, and not fully grown. If the truth were known, it is probably in its early teens now and won't become fully grown for some time. But it is growing and developing. We'll try to keep you updated as it grows. If I compared it to a symphony, I would say that it came more as a motif and now is into the exposition and development section. The recapitulation and second, third, and fourth movements are yet to come. But the leitmotif has been sounded and will ring through the entire work in a cyclical effect.

Since I was sixteen years old, I have felt that God had His hand on my life. If you are not a believer, that's all right. But surely you will grant me the sincerity of my intentions. I went to a Baptist seminary and worked and gave concerts in some of the largest churches and cathedrals throughout the world, including Notre Dame in Paris.

At Notre Dame, I was conducting Palestrina's "Dies Sanctifictus" and during the concert, the bells started ringing. I almost lost my place because I could just see the hunchback of Notre Dame swinging back and forth on the bell rope. After the concert, the monsignor said to the crowd that had gathered around, "You came as tourists. After hearing this, may you leave as pilgrims."

We also sang at Saint Mark's Cathedral in Venice. We climbed the heights. However, a few years ago when I was divorced, the church didn't want me anymore. I had to find another way to be involved with people, because God wasn't through with me yet and I am a service-oriented person.

I heard someone say, "The church is the only organization that shoots its wounded.'' Anyway, I think that is why God gave me this concept as a vehicle for touching people because the other was taken away from me. No, I'm not telling you I'm perfect, but I am driven. If you can't identify with these thoughts, just use the concepts from a purely business standpoint. Is that okay?

That should explain where the idea came from and why I have fought so hard for the concept. You see, I make no money unless you are in my organization, whether you use the concept or not. I do care that you have the opportunity.

# Eleven

## You Can Leverage Time

Yes, we can now leverage time. We can clone ourselves and break the twenty-four-hour time barrier. That is why we get so many professionals in networking. You see, a physician can only see so many patients within a twenty-four-hour time period. He can only charge so much. After that, he begins to experience diminishing returns.

In the past, the maximum number of times we could show the plan in a week was six times. This meant you almost killed yourself working every night of the week except Sunday.

Now, with the Two-Minute Coffee Shop Presentation, you can effectively present the plan thirty-six to fifty times a week, even if you are employed elsewhere full-time.

### O. P. M.

We have all heard of O. P. M. (Other People's Money). That is a term used in real estate, where you use other people's money to finance your project. Some call it "nothing down." We've all seen the TV shows where these techniques are explained. They work, too. But it is one of the things that has the real estate market in the mess that it is in now. Somebody's got to pay the piper.

In networking, we use O. P. T. (Other People's Time). Doesn't it stand to reason that, if you have one hundred people in your network merchandising for one hour a week, all other things being equal, you could make more money than if you alone worked one hour a week? You see, if I understand this correctly (and I think I do), you get a little bit from what they do. The further away from you they are in the group, the less you make, but you still make something.

Wasn't it Archimedes who said, "If I had a lever long enough, I could move the world"?

## Time Is Not Your Friend

We may be able to leverage time, but time is not our friend. If we live long enough, there is going to be an old person coming to live with us one of these days. All that old person is going to have is what we put away for him today. If that old person is going to live in dignity, he had better be prepared. Miller Williams said it best:

> . . . *I tell you, Tom, they will not let us pass.*
> *Madness, Old Age and Death, the rough boys*
> *who come down from the hills on bony mules*
> *know where we mean to go and they mean to stop us.*
> *They make a line in the dirt and stand there.*
> *Madness we can deal with. We know his moves.*
> *And Death's a sissy; he never comes full face*
> *when he's all by himself. He sneaks about. He hides.*
> *Old Age is slow but he never stops to rest.*
> *He can chase us down like a schoolyard bully*
> *and sit on our chests until we barely breathe*
> *while Death creeps close to put out his fist and*
> *hit us. . . .*

I know some people who are in their sixties, seventies, and even eighties who built multilevel empires during their middle age. Old age still caught them, but he didn't catch them broke. They live very enviable life-styles.

# Twelve

## Become a Student
## of the Business

Once you comprehend the concept of network marketing, decide to get involved in it, and become a student of it, your whole perspective begins to change. You begin to sense the urgency of how time can work for you and not against you. You shed the "quick fix" and begin to lay down long–term plans.

I am told the verbal portion of the brain is the strongest. I begin to teach my distributors early to say, "I'm in for life." That takes care of the day-to-day decisions and most of the major ones as to commitment. I am not talking about burning bridges, like quitting your job or some foolhardy decision like that. Simply this: "I'm in for the duration."

### There's No Logical Reason Not to Do It

As you study this business, you discover there is no logical reason not to do it. You begin to realize that anyone can build the business if you choose to help them. A person who might not have all the talents needed may have an uncle who is a dentist. He can get an appointment with the uncle for the two of you. But the uncle wouldn't give you or me the time of day if we called him without his nephew's influence. If the dentist gets in, the nephew with few talents benefits from the talents of his uncle. Are you beginning to see how it works?

There is another aspect of this business that comes into play if you are in it long enough to enjoy its benefits. Some people are ready to build the first week they are in it, but some require an incubation period. This may vary from weeks to years. If we try to birth some of these distributors during their incubation period, sometimes we get a stillbirth.

I guess the best way to illustrate this is: It takes nine months to have a baby, and getting nine women pregnant won't make it happen in a month.

## Acclimation

Skiers and mountain climbers have long been aware that you must become acclimatized before scaling the heights. Even those who climbed Mount Everest in order to ski down it took five days after the first major ascent, to allow their bodies to become adjusted to the thin air. In spite of this, six of them lost their lives.

I don't know why it is so hard for some of us to understand that many distributors, especially professionals, require a period of time in which to become acclimated to network marketing.

You understand that I am making a distinction between becoming acclimated and remaining in some warming hut and never attempting the peak. The road to success is paved with many convenient parking places and warming huts.

I've learned not to prejudge people in this business. They'll surprise you every time. Of all the Direct Distributors in my organization, I only personally picked out one. The others showed up downline. I missed it on almost every one. Some of those I picked fizzled out.

In my company, we use the term Direct Distributors. Other companies call them vice-presidents or something else. In simplest terms, I am talking about that level of accomplishment where a person breaks away from his sponsor and begins to deal directly with his company. I hope your company pays you an override when you help develop a Direct or vice-president. My company does.

## What Does It Take to Be Successful in Networking?

I think consistency is the most important thing. It is better to do a little bit every day or once a week consistently than it is to go in big spurts. Remember the story of the hare and the tortoise. I tell folks it doesn't take much of a man or woman to do networking, but it takes everything there is in that person to do it.

When I made Direct Distributor, I was invited to go to corporate headquarters in Ada, Michigan, for an all-expense-paid seminar. There were six large bus loads of new Direct Distributors there. I rode on a different bus from the hotel to the plant and back every day. I wanted to meet them all and find out the secret of what made each a Direct. I wanted to look them over and look into their eyes and find out what a Direct looked like, so I could spot them in the future.

I walked up and down the aisles of those buses and looked them right in the eyes. You know what I discovered? Nothing in common. Some were fat and some skinny. Some were tall and some short. A few even spoke languages other than English. There were professionals and nonprofessionals. Some were rich and some poor. Some were shy and some gregarious, singles and couples, single marrieds, educated and uneducated. Some were good-looking and some were not so good-looking. In fact, one fellow looked like he'd been whipped with an ugly stick. I couldn't find any common thread by looking at them.

Probably the thing I learned most from that experience is that you can't judge a book by its cover. You just can't tell by looking at a person what he can or will do. What was the name of that country-and-western song that said, "I'm just an old chunk of coal, but I'm gonna be a diamond someday"?

If you'll become a student of this business—a Michelangelo, if you please—you'll discover that there is a *Pietà* in every stone.

## Impression Without Expression Equals Depression

When I used to go to rallies, the speakers would say, "Work smart, not hard." I would get the speaker off in the corner, thinking he was going to give me the secrets, and ask, "How do you work smart, not hard?"

They would say, "Listen to tapes, show the plan six nights a week, go to rallies like this one, support your center, dream, and have a goal." This was and is good advice, but it was like firing an information shotgun; there was no focus. I think most of us need to zero in a little closer. I needed to know how to fire an information rifle. It seemed that my people did, too.

I would go home from these meetings so high I could fly. I was like the fellow who ran out and jumped into the cab. "Where to?" the cabbie asked. "Anywhere. I have business in all directions," the fellow answered.

Don't you agree that impression without expression equals depression? No wonder people quit faster than we could sponsor them.

## Knowledge Is Powerful

Knowledge is powerful. If I just get you pumped up with enthusiasm and dreams without the knowledge of what to do, the first time your sister-in-law pokes at you, she'll burst your balloon. That is why I tell people, "I'd rather you didn't talk to anyone until you have listened to your first four training tapes. Then I want you to go with me to help me and one of your upline sponsors sponsor someone at the coffee shop for you." There are exceptions to this, but the quickest way I can lose a distributor is for that lady to go out and start talking before she is trained. If she gets put down, she usually won't go back for a second dose. She'll say, "I don't need this." Especially if she doesn't.

I don't care if it is six weeks before they sponsor anyone or sell products, as long as they are coming to training. I tell my new distributors and prospects, "If Jesus took thirty years preparing and three years ministering, it's not a bad example for us."

## Be a Professional

By telling them to start using the products your company markets, you help them become knowledgeable about your merchandise, so they can speak from firsthand experience. But by telling them to take some time to get trained, you remove the "fast buck" aspect from it. I tell people, "If you decide not to join our network, that's okay. The timing might not be right, or any number of reasons. I just want you to appreciate the professional way in which you were treated. That way, if you ever do decide to get into networking, you'll think of me. And you won't mind bringing your banker, doctor, minister, or attorney to look at the business, because you know I won't try to embarrass them or you by pressing too hard."

I do try to close, but I don't press. You must ask for a decision, because they usually won't ask you. Closes are fun. It's like a cat and mouse game. You see, if you are showing the plan five or six times a day, you are not as anxious about any one individual. I just play the odds; some will join you and some won't.

## Once You've Let Them Sniff the Cork, Don't Take the Jug and Run Home

I tell people, "I'm looking for people who want to help me and let me help them, right now, to build a large network marketing business through which we can merchandise products." Sometimes they'll offer this or that reason why they don't think they want to join me. When they do, I write it down. Then I say, "Would there be any reason other than these that would keep you from joining me?" Then we discuss each. If they are legitimate reasons, they won't join you no matter what. If there is a misconception, explaining will help.

I heard a Diamond Direct say one day, "When people say no, they usually don't mean no. They mean 'I don't understand enough to say yes.' " Once you've let them sniff the cork, don't take the jug and run home.

No matter what their objection is, after we have talked about it, I just say, "If it ain't you, that's all right. I'm looking for those who want to build now. Don't worry about it. Maybe the time will be better in six months." Then I put them on my "I'll get you yet" list, but I don't bug them. I do give them a tape and a catalog to take home with them, and I set a time to meet them for coffee a few days later to pick up my tape and catalog. Don't take it personally when people decide not to join you. I heard a preacher say one time, "I just deliver the message. God provides the increase."

We've sat there for about thirty minutes and no one is the worse for wear. During that time, I peddle my wares and weave my magic. If they won't weave, I can't "weave 'em." I just do what one of my Crown friends from California teaches his distributors to do. When I get back to my car, I just yell as loudly as I can, "Next!"

## Expert Opinion

I advise people not to go out and talk to anyone about this business until they get trained because most of them know just enough to be dangerous. No matter to whom I am speaking, I say, "Even if you were the best heart surgeon in the world, I would give you the following advice. Can you take instructions? Two things: Keep your mouth shut and your ears open." They are like babes in the woods when they first join you.

What's the first thing a new distributor is going to do? Call his brother-in-law and get his expert opinion. Then they are going to call more experts—a banker and an attorney. Both of these "experts" are trained to look at the downside. They are usually not experts on multilevel, but some are. If it is a new company, you should have them check it out.

Let me tell you why you can't always take an expert's advice. Ask your uncle, banker, or attorney, "What do you stuff a turkey with?"

They'll say, "Bread crumbs, onions, celery, eggs, and giblets."

Now ask a turkey what you stuff a turkey with. He'll say, "Gobble, gobble, corn, gravel, and worms, gobble, gobble."

Who is the expert on stuffing a turkey? It depends on whether you are pitching or catching, doesn't it?

If you are going to ask someone about the network company you have joined, ask someone who has succeeded at it, not some uncle who failed.

# Thirteen

## Have Fun
## With Your Business

If you just get "eat up" with your business, you'll have more fun with it, especially if you know where to go next. So many people don't know what to do next. As a result, in their enthusiasm, they make fools out of themselves, get depressed, and quit. That doesn't need to happen, now. Go build three teams seven-deep and teach each of them to try to market two hundred dollars worth of products a month. But have fun doing it.

I have a minister friend whom I once asked how he got so excited and had so much fun with his sermons. He said: "I read myself full. I pray myself hot. God strikes a match, and I glow."

If you are prepared, you'll glow. And "when you're on the go, you've got the glow." If you are prepared, there's hardly anything that you can do wrong, so get out there and try your hand and "shoot up amongst 'em."

### Fire Your Best Shot

The reason most people won't work at this business isn't a lack of ability. In my opinion, they are not sure they could tell a prospect what to do if he did join them. They can read, can't they? If you are convinced that your network company is legitimate, try doing these three things, and you might get something going. After you have told your prospect what you know and have fired your best shot, give him these three things:

1. A copy of your company's sales and marketing plan, so he can take it home and study it

2. A sample of some of your company's products or a pamphlet about the services it offers

3. Your copy of this book or one that explains networking and a tape about your business.

Next, make an appointment to get back together with him, to see how he liked the samples and the concept. Then take him to a group meeting somewhere, so he can be around the kind of people you've been telling him about. What have you got to lose?

## Open Your Eyes

I was talking to a fellow one day, and I told him if he would devote three to five years, part-time, giving his best effort to this business, he might eventually replace his present income. He looked at me and said, "Man, in five years I'd be forty-three years old."

I looked at him for a minute and said, "How old are you going to be in five years if you don't try it?"

If we don't make such a big deal of it in the early stages and let people grow into it, we won't run as many people off. The eagles you can't hold down anyway. They'll take it away from you very quickly. They say, "Even a blind hog will find an acorn every now and then." I say, "If he's got his eyes open, he'll find more acorns." Open your eyes to the possibilities.

One evening I was at the home of one of my distributors who is an attorney. We'd had coffee shop meetings all day and had invited a number of people over to a meeting at his home, to take a closer look. After he and I explained our business to them in more detail, we broke up to let the people have refreshments and visit with one another. I was having a ball when a lady came over and asked me if I would talk to a friend whom she had brought to the meeting.

I am a teacher and can't talk without writing, so we made our way over to the chalkboard. The prospect worked as a teacher's helper.

I asked her, "Can you see why your friend and I are so high on this business?"

"Yes, but it's not for me."

"I was just wondering, would there be some reason why not?"

She said, "Oh, I don't know. I just don't have any dreams, and I could never do that." I told her that her friend and I would help her so she wouldn't have to build a business by herself. She got a faraway look in her eyes and said, "I've never had anything, and I've never seen any way that I could. I don't have any dreams."

I'm not that much into dreams without reality, but I thought I'd try something. She appeared genuinely interested but all bound up in what appeared to be fear of failure. So I took the marker and started writing on the board, all three of us oblivious to the others milling about the room. I said, "Mrs. Jones, let's see what it would take to make you dream. Would it be a new car?"

"No."

"Would it be a new washing machine? Or a new house?"

"No. I just don't have any dreams."

I said, "Mrs. Jones, your eyes were made for looking at the *Mona Lisa* and gazing at the *Venus de Milo* at the Louvre in Paris. Your eyes were made for looking at the Pyramids of Egypt as you sit astride a camel. Your eyes were made for looking at the Sphinx and gazing on King Tut's tomb. You're only going this way once. These things are not just for rich people. What would it mean for your child to stand up in Social Studies and say, 'I've ridden a *faluka* down the Nile River. I've stood at what is left of the Colossus of Rhodes that straddles the entrance to the city and used to welcome weary travelers, much as our Statue of Liberty does as she says, "Give me your tired, your poor, your huddled masses yearning to breathe free!" ' "

She yelled out, "I want to do it, but I don't have the money."

She made arrangements to get the less than one hundred dollars. Some of her friends helped her. But there is an important hidden point here.

## People Have Two Reasons for Doing Things

They taught us this when I sold Bibles door-to-door for Southwestern Publishing Company in Nashville, Tennessee. People have two reasons for doing things: One is the one that sounds good; the other is the real reason. You are probably as aware as I am that the thing that keeps many people from getting involved is the hundred dollars (less than that, actually). Many people are driving nice cars, wearing nice clothes, living in nice houses, but they are about to have their utilities cut off.

We tell people to "try our business and give it your very best and be teachable for sixty to ninety days, and study the business from the inside. Then, if you aren't pleased with the progress you and I have made, and if I haven't given you the help I told you I would give you, we'll go our separate ways as friends. About all you would have lost at that point would be a little time." But you had better get after it and get them going. I'm betting my sixty to ninety days against their sixty to ninety days that together we can get a fire kindled. We may not get a symphony written during that time, but perhaps we can settle on the motif for it.

I think you need to be fair with people. When you deal with their emotions and dreams, it is best to be careful. People know when you are using them. They can spot a phony in a minute. Women especially seem to have a sixth sense about that.

I think God loves us all. But I think He has a special place in His heart for women who live alone, the elderly, children, the sick, and the homeless. I take special care when dealing with them. Don't you agree? Jesus said, ". . . Inasmuch as ye have done it unto one of the least of these my brethren, ye have done it unto me" (Matthew 25:40). You'd be better off with a rattlesnake in your bosom than to hurt one of these. He doesn't always settle His accounts in September, like the farmers do, but there comes a payday, so let's all "tote fair."

# **Fourteen**

## How to Spot a Phony Network Marketing Pitch

Many network marketing companies are like cockroaches: They mess up more than they eat. One of the things I should caution you about is that there are a lot of phonies out there extolling the virtues of their companies. If you have been around the network marketing business very long, you are probably as aware as I am of the opportunities for abuse.

### The Warts and Beauty Marks of Network Marketing Companies

As I talk with you about my experiences with networking, if I can't help, I don't want to hurt. I will tell you about the warts as well as the beauty marks. That way, if you decide to get into it, you'll at least go in with your eyes open. If you don't, you'll know what it is you're not getting into and why. Folks can't trick you with their phony phrases then.

Let me illustrate. One of the myths I want to expose is the one that says, "Networking is an easy way to get rich quick." Now let's use our common sense for a minute. (When I taught at the university level, we were always going to offer a course in common sense; but we never could find anyone to teach it.)

Don't you and I know a lot of people who are or were in networking? Now, I'm not talking about someone about whom we've heard. I'm talking about someone you know. Do you know anyone who has gotten rich quick in it? What is quick? Let's say six months to a year. No, let's say two years. I don't know a one, do you? I hear about them, but when I check out the story, it is usually just hype. If there were that many people getting rich quickly in network marketing, wouldn't you or I have run across one of them by now? I am out there in the coffee shops every day.

I did meet two individuals who were with a new company that was less than a year old. They told me they were making $100,000 a month. I asked to see copies of their checks. They said, "We can't show them to you because we haven't gotten paid in two months. The company can't meet its bonus payments. We are waiting on this rich Arab to come to town who is going to infuse the company with ten million dollars so the company can make its bonus payments."

I said, "What will happen if this rich person from another country does not loan your president the ten million dollars to pay back bonuses?"

They said, "Our company will file for Chapter Eleven at ten on Friday morning."

That is a sad story, isn't it? They were good men. They'd flown high and now could only be embarrassed for their friends and families.

But they didn't learn. They were flying out to the West Coast that afternoon to meet with someone else and move their distributors to a new cosmetic or vitamin company that some movie star had started.

But let's talk about companies hat have stayed around a couple of years or more, including Amway, Shaklee, Avon, and so forth. I don't know of anyone personally who has gotten rich in two years, and I've been around the best of them.

I've been in the networking business for a little over three years. I have neither the largest nor the smallest business. I certainly haven't gotten rich, and I'm at least average. I know several people who have gotten rich in networking, but I don't know of any who did it all that quickly. I do think you can probably do it quicker in networking than in most other businesses, especially since you can do it with an investment of less than one hundred dollars.

I think the best networking companies are those that will teach you how to make a couple of hundred dollars your first or second month. If you can learn to do that, you can learn to multiply it.

The people I know who have made any sizeable money quickly in networking didn't make it on their network, but rather on some large personal sales. The more personal business you do, obviously, the more you make. You don't have to sell many large items—such as pay phones, water-treatment systems, or security systems—to make as much as you do on your regular job.

## Catchphrases That Should Be Red Flagged

You can spot some phony network marketing companies by their catchphrases. When you hear one of these, throw up a red flag and hightail it.

1. *"Get in on the ground floor."*

This is the most innocent sounding and yet potentially the most deadly of all their siren calls. Their pitch is this: "Get in now while it is only one thousand dollars, because next month it is going to be five thousand dollars."

Your answer to them should be, "Let's see, now. What you are telling me is that it is not going to be as good for my friends and relatives as it was for me." If you get in on the ground floor, your friends and relatives may wind up with the bottom of the outhouse, and that stinks. If you are going to get into networking, get into a company where everyone begins on the ground floor, even if it is thirty years old.

2. *"Get into my new network company because that 'old' company that has been around so long has already saturated the market. You would have to have gotten in twenty years ago to have done any good."*

When I first got into the Amway business, I told my sponsor, "I wish I had gotten in twenty years ago when you did."

He said, "Well, you didn't! Besides, they only had one product then and now they have thousands and are in forty-four countries and territories."

I still wish I had been sitting in the boardroom when Rich and Jay started the company. Boy, think where I'd be. I know now that I wouldn't be anywhere just from having been there. I would still have had to build my own business. Being in early is of little consequence if you don't build your own organization.

I hope you understand that I am bragging on the company rather than myself when I tell you that I know of three other people besides myself who last year, for their first year, did more volume than the entire Amway Corporation did its first year in business ($500,000). If the market were saturated, we couldn't have done that, could we? I'll bet if the truth were known, there were people in other legitimate networking companies who did, also.

Does that seem significant to you? That you could start now and in a year be as big as Amway was its first year?

3. *"You can buy your way in as a vice-president or regional director."*

This is called "inventory loading" and is not only unethical, but I believe it is also illegal. A legitimate company will have some sort of rule, such as a 70/30 rule, which says you must have marketed at least 70 percent of the stock you purchase.

4. *"If you can't sell your inventory, you can always use it."*

This is their stock answer to inventory loading. Ask them these questions and satisfy yourself. "How could I ever use up twenty-five-hundred dollars worth of gold chains, vitamins, or cosmetics?" "Will you take inventory back if I can't sell it?" If the answer is no, your relatives are going to get a lot of health-food mixes for a lot of Christmases and birthdays. A good company does not want its products sold at a garage sale; they'll take them back. If the new company won't, be careful.

5. *"This company is only six months old and is growing by leaps and bounds. Its leader has had many years' experience in networking."*

Caution is the word. What is your obvious question? "With what company has he had this vast experience?" In many cases, though not all, he got in trouble with legal agencies, changed the label on his product, changed the name of his company and the stickers on his suitcase, and moved across the state line to begin his *modus operandi* with a new group of suckers.

I decided that if I were going to give three to five years of my life to a networking company, I wanted to be sure it was going to be around in three to five years. The best assurance, though not the only one, is that if it was around three to five years ago, its chances of staying around are better than if it wasn't in existence five years ago.

6. *"This company and its products are endorsed by Joe and Jane Athlete, Jim Senator, Mary Pop-Singer, and Jesus Himself. Our products will even cure pregnancy, according to Dr. Quackery, who got his degree by correspondence from Airmail University."*

If the deal is so solid, a simple business explanation will do. A knowing business person with average intelligence can ascertain for himself or herself.

All the product needs is a label approved by the Food and Drug Administration.

I heard an outstanding minister speak to a group of young preachers. He said, "You can't get into a pulpit and whoop and holler loud enough to make up for the time you forgot to spend on your knees before you started."

Because I have a church background, I have to speak and write with illustrations I know. What I am saying is: You can't get enough endorsements from good people to make a bad deal better. You can't develop enough enthusiasm and hold enough rallies to fool reasonably intelligent people with an inferior product for very long.

7. *"We'll draft on your account and send you some products every month. That way we guarantee that everyone does his volume."*

You can shear a sheep several times, but you can only skin him once. You may sucker an "ole boy" once, but about the second or third time, he feels skinned.

This is the story of the donkey and the stick. The donkey wouldn't move, so they popped him with a stick. The donkey didn't like that too much.

It seems to me that if there were a way to hang a carrot out in front of the donkey, he'd move along better, and I know he'd like it better. What about a plan that says, "If you'll do so much volume, you'll participate in a bonus structure." That sounds better to me.

8. *"No. Our company isn't international yet, but you wouldn't be interested in that. We'll let our international agents handle that when we are. It's too complicated, anyway."*

If your company has your best interest at heart, it will find a way to allow you to participate in its international market and protect your downline there.

9. *"I know this lady who got into a new networking company when it started six months ago and is making one hundred thousand dollars a month. I've seen her checks."*

The Better Business Bureau says, "If it sounds too good to be true, it probably is." There's nothing wrong with getting rich, but I never saw a get-rich-quick scheme that didn't ultimately bite most of those involved. I'm a sucker for a deal, and I've fallen for some of them myself.

If someone actually has a check for that kind of money, ask him to show you a few others who have them, too. If he can't give you other people in your area, chances are that one or two are skinning the rest of you. Also, you know the profits are probably not being shared in an equitable fashion with the downline. It is going to be top-heavy and fall over. You see, you have no way of knowing if that check is a commission on inventory he has purchased in order to buy out a title or territory.

I met one man whose new networking company was in trouble. I was showing him how he could make one thousand to two thousand dollars a month.

He said, "Why are you showing me that? I'm making one hundred thousand dollars a month." I sat there and looked at him. He said, "When I get paid. They've not been able to pay us our bonuses for the past two months. Also, I had to spend fifty thousand dollars to make one hundred thousand dollars." He had leased a building for ten thousand dollars a month, hired a full staff and a fancy phone setup. He not only lost the one hundred thousand dollars a month, but also was saddled with the ten-year leases on the building and equipment. I work out of my car, have a twenty-five dollar answering machine and no staff, and did over five hundred thousand dollars in business last year.

If I could say anything to you that would help you not be skeptical, but careful, it would be this: It has been my experience that there is not as much money in the networking business in the early stages as most people have been led to believe. A legitimate company will tell you that it takes three to five years to begin to make serious money in networking.


10. *"The XYZ Networking Company just went bankrupt. The president of that company is starting a new company with a new product. He'll be here Monday, and you can clean up if you get in before he moves all of his other distributors into this new company."*

Need I say more? But you would be surprised by the good people who get taken in by this ruse.

I don't know why people fall for such obviously blatant trickery. I guess part of it is because people are gullible. Some do want the fast buck. Maybe it is the hard times in which we now find ourselves. But sometimes it consists of good people at the wrong place at the wrong time. Many times it is because someone is legitimately looking for a vehicle on which to pin his hopes and dreams, and that "ain't bad." But sometimes the outcome is catastrophic.

The best advice I could give you is to join a company that has a long track record, at least five years or longer, if you can find one. Be careful that it is the *company* that has the track record, and not the *individual*. You see, an individual may have done well with an older established networking company and then flop on his own. The reason is probably obvious to you. The older established company had to have known how to run a networking business on sound business principles in order to survive, whereas the individual may merely possess the talents of a promoter or salesman. These are good talents, but not enough to qualify one to begin a company.

11. *"It is a new company."*

Being a new network marketing company is usually the kiss of death. In no other business does the word *new* so signify the likely ultimate demise of a company as in networking. You might ask, "Why? Weren't Shaklee, Herbalife, Avon, or even Amway new once?" Of course, and someone may someday come along and outdo all of them. But examine the records of networking companies. I understand there have been over four hundred network companies that have said, "We are just like Amway, only better," but who are not around anymore.

What does that tell you? If you are going to get into one, your odds are better if you don't get into a new one.

Developing a business within an established networking business is very simple, a lot of fun, and inexpensive. But the

119

intricacies of starting a networking company are far more complex than the average promoter, salesman, or entrepreneur realizes.

If it is touted as a new network company, you had better stay away unless you have personal legal knowledge, know corporate intricacies, Federal Trade Commission laws, finance, marketing, interstate commerce, advertising, research and development, and international law.

12. *"My company has only one product. You don't get confused."*

If the company has only one product, that doesn't mean you should avoid it, but it probably means the company is short-sighted. That doesn't matter unless you want to sign up with a company for the long haul. How would you like to have been selling buggy whips when the automobile came out?

## Hold on to Your Billfold and Your Reputation

I don't mean to be skeptical, but I'd certainly be careful not to get involved in networking with an unproven company. If one of the above baited hooks is dangled in your face, throw up a mental red flag until you check it out, and hold on to your billfold and your reputation. Sometimes the loss of your reputation and credibility with friends, family, and clients far outweighs the $10,000 (or whatever figure they ran at you) investment fee they wanted.

Many people are led up the primrose path by being told, "Your family and friends will benefit from your success. You can provide for them when you succeed, whether they join you or not." This is true if it is a good deal with a good company. But it won't make a bad deal good.

## Would You Recommend Some Good Network Companies?

No. But there are some good ones out there. I suggest you apply the concepts discussed in this book as well as your common sense and a few basic business principles, find one with ideas and principles with which you agree, and jump in. It's a lot of fun, not very expensive, brings a lot of recognition, and you can do it part-time.

Many people get into networking not so much for the money as for the recognition. You are rewarded at every level. Some have said about recognition, "Babies cry for it, and men die for it."

## Have You Ever Thought About Starting Your Own Network Marketing Business?

No. Every now and then someone will say to me, "Why don't you start your own networking company?" I say, "Why? The company with which I am associated has done all the work in organizing a company, has the history, the success, the computer for records, and the products and services. How could I possibly beat that?" And besides that, I don't know how.

Sometimes someone will come to me and say, "I want to start a networking company. Will you help me?"

I tell them, "I only know how to build one. I don't know how to start one. That's not my cup of tea." I advise them to get a good attorney on multilevel marketing and then run their documents by the Federal Trade Commission prior to opening for business. And then forget it. Perhaps that will keep them from running afoul of the law.

It is amazing how many professional people will risk their entire profession by getting into some fly-by-night networking company. Money leaves a trail, and if the whole thing is illegal, you can imagine the consequences when your name appears on the court docket.

With a network marketing company, there is much opportunity for misrepresentation, both intentional and unintentional. Get with a company that has been around at least five years. By then, they will have worked out some of the worst kinks. I'm just saying, use good business sense, because you can lose more than you have. How many people do you know right now who, because of poor business decisions, intentional or unintentional, would give anything just to be even?

## Forewarned Is Forearmed

In the third week of January 1987, I was presenting our program to one of my new distributor's prospects at a coffee shop. Prior to the appointment, my new distributor called and said that her prospect would come to hear our program if I would go with them to hear about a "new" network marketing program where they were giving away cars for one hundred dollars if you would just sign up three people.

I processed it through my red-flag test and said, "No, thank you." I explained that the worst thing you can say about a new company in network marketing is that it is new. The meeting they wanted me to attend was on the following Tuesday evening.

That Tuesday on the 10:00 P.M. news in Dallas, there were live camera shots of the meeting being busted up, the people handcuffed and hauled off to jail for "pyramidding." My distributor and her new distributor had not gone. They called and thanked me for alerting them to the dangers. Some of their friends weren't so lucky. They said, "Why doesn't someone tell people about these scams?" Forewarned is forearmed.

## If You Fail, Let it Be You Who Failed and Not the Company

In all fairness, I should tell you that just joining a successful company will not guarantee you will be a success. But at least you won't fail because the company did.

You may have been in so many network marketing companies that you are sick of the term and feel like a multilevel prostitute. But at least you were out there trying.

What I am saying is, you can't possibly succeed if the company doesn't. And you might not, even if you get with a good company. But you'll never know if it is the proper vehicle for your talents unless you stop shooting yourself in the foot and try with a solid, legitimate company.

One physician friend of mine told me that before he got into network marketing, he thought he was too good for it. He got involved. Later he said that he wondered if he was good enough for it.

Looks simple.

Is simple.

Ain't easy.

# Fifteen

## Stored Time
## Equals Freedom

If freedom is our ultimate goal in networking, let's begin to formulate some concepts about that. Could we all agree that freedom is being able to do what you want, with whom you want, where you want, and when you want? Could we also agree that the thing keeping us from this freedom is a job where we spend our time in order to get the money to do these things? And there still doesn't seem to be enough money?

If our job or occupation is taking most of our time and is not producing enough money for us to afford to go and come as we please, we have reached at least one obvious conclusion.

Money is stored time. Stored time equals freedom. Let me illustrate. I say to you, "Let's go to Hawaii in the morning for two weeks." You have the freedom to go. You reply, "But I have a boss and a job." Do you see that I am talking about a different kind of freedom?

### But How Will I Get My Sales Force to Arizona?

Many salesmen, and others who built large organizations in insurance or automobile dealerships, thought they were storing time and were going to find the pot at the end of the rainbow; they only found a cesspool.

Have you ever heard this story? Joe goes to work for DFG Computer Sales. He builds up a large sales force and leads the nation in sales. The company calls him in and says, "You've done so well, we're going to make you a vice-president, give you a hundred dollar a month raise, and move you to Arizona."

Joe says, "But I don't want to move to Arizona, and besides that, how would I get all my salespeople to move out there?"

"They're not your salespeople. They belong to the company."

"I still don't want to move to Arizona."

"Take it or leave it."

The story sounds all too familiar, doesn't it? Here's another true story with another company.

Sue leads the country in sales, and her company calls her in and says, "You've done fantastic. You've developed such a large client base that we now feel your territory needs to be cut in half. Meet Jim Nephew, just out of college, who is going to take over the other half of your territory."

Sue's options: Tell them where to stick it, and start over with another company, or accept it and say to herself, *I'll teach them. I won't grow as much next year.*

My network marketing company said, "If you help a person build an organization to Direct Distributor, when he breaks away from you, we'll pay you a 3 percent willable, inheritable bonus on that individual's volume as long as he remains at least at that level." Not too shabby. That's where the freedom comes in.

In fact, in networking, the larger your business becomes, the less work is involved and the more freedom you have. Once a person gets to a certain level of merchandising, breaks away from the sponsor, and deals directly with the company, he begins to realize that he can build as many groups as he wants to. He can clone himself and break the twenty-four-hour time barrier.

## Is It Possible to Store Enough Time to Eventually Become Wealthy in Network Marketing?

If it isn't "get rich quick," can people ultimately get rich? Many have. I haven't—yet. Just like on television, where we only hear the bad news, we often hear only bad news about networking. More often we hear about the fraudulent companies. Many of these companies didn't intend to cheat anyone in the beginning; they just didn't understand networking.

Be that as it may, many of the finest people in the world are in networking. They are doctors, janitors, attorneys, truck drivers, factory workers, farmers, nurses, and housewives. Some of these people are wealthy beyond our wildest dreams. You don't hear about them because they only move about inside their giant worldwide empires. Some of these people are so powerful that when they speak, presidents listen. In fact, they hobnob with governors, senators, presidents, and kings. Many of them keep a low public profile, and it would be virtually impossible to get an appointment with them, not because they are so busy, but because they are so powerful and have so much stored time that it's hard to find them.

## Why Would My Banker or Doctor Be Interested in Getting Into Networking?

Occasionally someone will say, "Why would my banker be interested in getting into networking?"

I say, "Is he still working? If he is, he's still interested in making money." He may not be interested in networking, but he will talk to you about making money.

Another might say, "Why would my doctor be interested?" Just call him up and say, "Doctor Jones, is it true that most physicians are making a good living for their wives and children but are killing themselves?"

He'll usually laugh and say, "How did you know?" You can then tell him a little about the products you merchandise and tell him you want to get together with him over a cup of coffee, to see if you can't clone him.

I usually find the banker more interested in making money and the doctor more interested in stored time or cloning himself.

I try to recruit anyone who *wants* more, rather than *needs* more. I don't care whether he or she is a professional or not. If they are not employed somewhere, I don't usually spend much time with them. I try to recruit professionals because I don't have to spend as much time training them. I learned a long time ago that, "If you are going to launch the big ships, you've got to get in the deep water." I think the appeal of stored time gets a real hold on them.

## Strong as a Mule's Breath

This would probably be a good time to tell you that if you have three strong friends, three dentists, or three children of age, I suggest you personally sponsor them as heads of your three legs. This is an exception to building one leg seven-deep before starting the second leg. We've taught this exception from the first. The reason for this is that in the beginning, we are only talking about three names, and it doesn't sound that significant.

But in the long-term scheme of things, we may be talking about three different empires.

You need to decide the goal you wish to achieve in your networking business. Obviously, if you are in Amway, your long-range goal is to have at least six qualified legs for what is called Diamond. That provides a lot of stored time. By way of interest, the entire Amway Corporation is built on only five legs.

We usually teach people to build three legs at a time. However, if you know six "hosses," sponsor them personally and let them get after it. It has been my experience, though, that a lot of strong people with worlds of potential don't become strong in this business until you help them. I don't care if they are as strong as a mule's breath; the stronger they are, the quicker you must help them get some success.

If you opt for this exception, you must get with them immediately and teach them how to clone themselves and give them the basic concepts. Otherwise, they may sit there and die on you. By the time you have time to help them, and you call them up and say so, you may find you are going to help them find where they buried the starter kit, rather than help them open for business.

## What If McDonald's Had to Personally Know All Their Customers?

The easiest way to keep from depersonalizing your distributors is to treat everyone as though you personally sponsored them until you get a Direct Distributor in the leg.

But you can't be buddies with all of them. Just imagine if the Holiday Inn or McDonald's had to personally know everyone before they rented them a room or sold them a hamburger. They couldn't do much business, could they? I think it is important that we start treating our network businesses like real businesses.

A good approach to someone who runs a hamburger place, a doughnut shop, or a motel might be this: "Do you have a lot of time or freedom from your job? Are you doing anything to store more time?"

## You and I Will Build the Network Together

When I speak with a new person about how we store time, in order to get his belief going, I ask him, "Do you think I know how to build this business?"

He usually says, "Yes, but I could never do what you have done."

I say, "Well, if I can build it by myself, don't you think you and I could build it together?"

He usually says, "I see what you mean. I won't have to do it by myself. The last time I got sponsored, I put my starter kit under the bed and never saw my sponsor again. The kit didn't hatch, either. I think I could do it with you helping me." That's team sponsoring at its best. I then use the close on them that my sponsor used on me. He said, "Let's get the paperwork out of the way."

## What Do You Get Out of Helping Me Build a Team?

I think that most folk agree that, all other things being equal, it takes about seventy-five to a hundred distributors in your organization in order to get and hold enough volume to become a Direct Distributor. (Mere numbers of distributorships, without volume, are meaningless. Obviously, you must teach them to merchandise. But you can't teach them until you recruit them.)

Why would I be willing to help you build your teams? Is it just because I like you? I probably do like you, but you would be suspicious of that motive, since I may have only known you about a week.

Is it because I am such a magnanimous person and have nothing else to do? Someone said, "It sounds like a welfare system, to me."

I say, "No, it's more like the story of *The Little Red Hen*. She did all the work, but then she got to invite whom she wanted to the banquet."

The reason I will help you is very simple. As I said earlier, my company will pay me a 3 percent override on your business as soon as I can get you to the Direct Distributor level. It will continue to pay me that amount, which is willable and inheritable, as long as you are at the Direct Distributor level. They pay me directly, and it comes from the company; it doesn't come from you. I can build these organizations, but I don't want to run them. As soon as I help you build your organization, you break away from me and deal directly with the company, and I can go play. That is where the freedom comes in. But I can't go play until I get you to Direct.

You might say, "That is well and good, but what if I quit after you have helped me to get to the Direct level? Then what do you get?" At that point, the organization just moves right back to me, and I get the bonus on the volume in your organization. I win if you stay, and I win if you quit. The same is true for you. I want you to stay because I don't want to run the organization. But if I have to, I am compensated financially. When you understand this part of networking and can implement it, you are no longer dependent on the ups and downs of personalities. You are in control.

What do I get out of helping you become a Direct Distributor? More stored time, and stored time equals freedom. I get freedom!

"What do you think we need to do first, in order to help me get to the Direct Distributor level and get you another three percent in stored time?"

Focus. We've got to hone in on one leg and catch it on fire and fan it until it is full-blown, red-hot, and ready to explode.

You can take a magnifying glass and get it at the right angle to the sun and burn a hole in a wooden desk. But if you move the magnifying glass around, it doesn't even create warmth—it just gets sunlight in people's eyes and irritates them.

You need to develop a thirst for this business that can only be quenched when we have focused enough fire on one aspect of the structure at a time that it culminates by popping out a brand-new Direct Distributor.

Syntax is the marshaling of words. By giving focus to one aspect of a structure at a time, we are able to marshal our distributors, creating a lever-and-fulcrum type of dynamic, helping us to both leverage and store time. This often causes a leg to implode and explode simultaneously, just like popcorn. Wow! Did I say that? You'd better listen; this is my best stuff.

# Pastoral
# Symphony

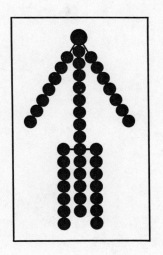

# Sixteen

## Camelot?

One of the beliefs that I had while building my organization was that once I got a rather large organization built, we would all live in peace, harmony, and love in the Utopia of Camelot. Oh, boy. When you are building and growing fast, some of your time and energy will be spent in putting out fires with some of your key leaders. Sometimes they will lock horns.

My sponsors pushed me out of the nest the day I was born. And boy, I flew. I was afraid I'd hit the ground.

### Give Them Space

If you are going to be big in this business, I think you must push some of your distributors out of the nest. One of the things that causes personality conflicts is simply that you have too many strong leaders still flailing around in the nest. My best advice is to give them some space and teach them to give one another space. Get away from one another and do your own thing until things cool down.

Sometimes I need time just to let my soul catch up with my body.

My upline Crown Ambassadors were giving a speech at a meeting I attended in New Mexico. They were describing the qualities of a good distributor within an organization. They said, "One of the most important things for a distributor to be is attitude dependable." I've thought about that statement many times. I think I would rather have that said of me than any other statement. I want distributors who are attitude dependable.

## When Two People Agree on Everything, You Don't Need One of Them

We should have the right to disagree with each other. When two people agree on everything, you don't need one of them. You must also provide a time when they can be with you, to let you know their disagreements as well as to rejoice with them. Not in public. Get your leadership together to discuss their concerns before they fester into full-blown standoffs.

Be careful not to label a distributor a troublemaker just because he or she works harder or smarter or more creatively than you do. Even network companies must provide a format for tapping the creative genius of their distributors and allowing them to disagree and make suggestions. A suggestion box would even help. A minority report, if you please. A good company leaves its operation open to abuse even with a board designed to represent its distributors. You see, each distributor must have a representative on such a board who is not in competition with him.

I once heard a discussion about democracy in action. The speaker said, "All it takes for tyranny to raise its ugly head is for good men to remain silent."

Just be fair with your distributors and provide a forum for them, either formally or informally. For the company, there must be a place where the "lamb and the lion" can lie down together without fear. If they can't, the lamb isn't going to get much sleep.

## Some People Shouldn't Be Sponsored

Not everyone is a sorehead; some people are "turned good." They wear well. Anybody would and could get along with them. Some have childish ways. Some distributors are just "plumb out of their gourds." I think some people never should have been sponsored. If he was a nut before he got in, he'll probably still be a nut. You may not have much to do with him getting in. He may have gotten in downline. But once he's in, you and I have to find a way to work with him.

Vince Lombardi said that one of the most difficult tasks in coaching was finding out how to deal with the diverse personalities on his football team. I can't tell you how to do the job, but I have a goal with mine. I want them to like themselves better when they are with me than when they are with anyone else. I am not always successful, but that's always my goal.

## There Was Tension at the Cross

For many of us, the highest expression of love ever made, and the most sacred moment, was at the Cross. And yet, would anyone deny that there was tension there, also? Even if your organization is full of love and caring, it is probably going to have some tension.

The only problem with most of us is that we just haven't lived long enough. If you stay in this business long enough and build big enough, you're going to have someone whom you helped become a Direct Distributor or vice-president turn and spit in your face, like a child in a rage who slaps his mother. The tendency is to lash back. But you and I must be emotionally stable for our group; although that doesn't keep it from hurting and breaking your heart, does it?

Sometimes you feel like they never even knew you at all. Do you ever get on your "pity pot"? Yeah, me, too. Sometimes I want to climb inside my emotional shell and sing Don William's country-and-western song about a fellow who lost his love, "She Never Knew Me At All." He and Anne Murray are my favorite singers. I know it doesn't have anything to do with network marketing, but I told you I have fun. Most of us take ourselves far too seriously.

You know what I like to do sometimes? Stop and talk to a guy who is riding around the airport or shopping mall in one of those motorized wheel chairs. I like to ask him how fast it goes and if he can "pop a wheelie" with it.

I guess we had better return to networking. I didn't want things to get too serious, though. Let some of the tension out. This is heavy stuff.

## Olive Branch

You have to be ready to reconcile with wayward distributors, just as Hosea had kept his love for Gomer faithful unto death, when her prostitution had landed her in slavery. He went to the auction block and bought her back for fifteen shekels of silver and a homer and a half of barley.

You must hold out an olive branch continuously to your distributors who may be mad at you; perhaps one of them heard you went to coffee with a person he is in disagreement with.

He may be like the fellow I heard about who quit going to

football games. Every time they huddled, he thought they were talking about him.

Some of your distributors whose businesses you have helped build will want to try their own wings. Let them. Don't hold them too closely; you may smother them. But stay next to them; you'll eventually have to wean them. In spite of all your best efforts, some will turn on you and blame you for their failings and take full credit for their successes. That goes with the territory. A part of this may just be human nature. I say, keep the yellow ribbon on the old oak tree. If you've treated them fairly and with dignity, they'll eventually come around. You may have to make the first move; you also may have to make the second and third.

But in the meantime, you know a little of how Jehovah must have felt when the children of Israel went after the false priests and yelled in His face: "I will go after my lovers, that give me my bread and my water, my wool and my flax, mine oil and my drink" (Hosea 2:5).

I don't know if God cries or not. But if He does, He must have as He spoke these words in reply: "It is I who taught Ephraim to walk. . . . Your loyalty is like a morning cloud, and like the dew which goes away early" (Hosea 11:3; 6:4 NAS).

You may have taught your distributors to walk by helping them build their legs. But at some point, you must let them try their wings. Only then will you know if you have truly succeeded.

Some will try to prostitute your teachings. They will be like Icarus, from ancient Greek mythology, who pinned wings to his back with wax. He flew higher and higher, mocking the sun gods with his newfound freedom and false sense of security. As he flew closer and closer to the heat, the wax melted, the wings dropped off, and he fell to his death.

At lunch with my sponsor one day, I was telling him about a distributor in another organization who had gone off on his own with some harebrained ideas. My sponsor said, "You can't prostitute this business and survive." How true. And yet it is one of the most forgiving businesses.

Others of your distributors will soar to new heights. Standing on your shoulders and the shoulders of your upline and other giants in the business, they will reach peaks you only dreamed of.

I have a way of getting them back down to earth, though. When they ask me, "How come it took you so long to make Direct?" I tell them, "I didn't have me helping me." Also, "I did it the traditional, competitive way."

I try to keep them humble, but I never clip their wings. You see, the better they do, the better we both do.

# **Seventeen**

# What Type
# of Personality Does Best
# at Networking?

$O$ne of the myths about network marketing is that you need to be a salesman or entrepreneur to be successful at it. Surprisingly enough, it has been my experience that salesmen do the worst. Why? A salesman is used to doing everything; he usually does not have the patience or leadership skills to develop a group. If you can find one who knows how to train and lead people, he'll go to the top. Most of them will say, "I don't need a network. I could sell a hundred of those chain saws myself."

I say, "Yes, and you'd have to do it again next month. What if you had a network of one hundred distributors who each sold one chain saw?"

## **Engineers, Attorneys, Pilots, and Architects**

I think the reason these people excel is not because of their personality types, but rather because of their knowledge and belief in structure. They can see the logic of it, if they see it at all. Many times an engineer will think he can't, because he thinks you need a "rah-rah" personality. But if you can get him to look at it, he'll see the logic.

Attorneys are taught to look at the downside of a deal, but if you can get him past his preconceived ideas about the negatives of networking, he'll usually see it. He may not join you, but he'll see it. My upline Crown Ambassador is a very soft-spoken attorney; if you were shooting salesmen, you wouldn't aim at him.

My sponsor is a very shy architect who turns red in the face when you ask him a question. Yet he is a Diamond and has several Diamonds and one Crown Ambassador in his business. His wife is the epitome of "Miss Culture."

Every now and then, someone will say to me, "I could never build an organization. I just couldn't do that. I don't have an outstanding personality."

Sometimes I get poetic and say, "If only the birds in the forest with the loveliest voices sang, it would be an awfully dull forest." I heard that somewhere. Then we get down to business.

## My Life-style Wouldn't Attract Anyone

Others will say, "If I were a successful businessman like you, I could build this business, too. But I'm not. I don't have the life-style to show people that it works."

I say, "Introduce them to your Direct or someone in the business who is successful in networking."

They respond, "But I wouldn't want to try to contact a successful businessman or woman until I have built a large, successful network. They wouldn't listen to me unless I had a large organization."

"Not so. Jesus never pastored a church. Yet every Christian

pastor teaches His concepts. You see, it isn't *you* that you are trying to sell; it is your company's program and products.''

## A Homemade Coffin

Sometimes when people tell me they don't have a life-style like mine, I think, *If they only knew.* The first two houses we ever lived in had dirt floors.

I remember when my little sister, Hetty Sue, died of pneumonia because we couldn't afford a doctor or medicine. We made a wooden coffin, put her in the trunk of my uncle's car, took her up into the Cherokee National Forest near the Old Maggie Mill, and buried her.

If you are going to tell me you are poor, you are talking my language. I'm knowledgeable on the subject of poor. I'm going to tell you how to get unpoor.

## Wealth Can Be Replaced

When people talk to me about wealth and life-style, I tell them, ''You can build wealth, and lose it, and build it again. But you can't do that with integrity. Mr. Jones, you have integrity, don't you? Let's market that.'' Then I quote this little poem:

> *When wealth is gone, little is gone.*
> *When health is gone, much is gone.*
> *When integrity is gone, all is gone.*

## Can You Fly a 747?

I say, ''Can you fly a 747?'' They usually say no. I say, ''If I gave you five thousand dollars for the name of each person who could fly one, do you think you could round up some names?''

Many people might not be able to do this business until they learned all about it, but they know people who already have all the necessary skills. They get paid whether they build it or get someone else to build it. Not as much in the second case, but something.

I sponsored my maintenance man, who had a fifth-grade education. He thought he couldn't build the business. In his organization he now has a Pearl and at least seven qualified Direct Distributors on one of his teams. Volume for that leg last year was over three hundred thousand dollars.

## Companies and Organizations Within Them Have Personalities

Assuming that you are with a sound, legitimate company, I think anyone who wants to can build a networking business. But some companies and some organizations within them offer their distributors more help than others. Some have fun with it, and some gripe and argue all the time. Some are very open, but some are very secretive. Nothing is wrong with any of these; you just need to find which personality type fits yours.

It's like denominations and churches within a particular denomination, synagogue, or temple. The same God may be ruler over all, but the personalities and abilities of the leaders differ vastly.

I think the day may have arrived, now that network marketing is so attractive, that people will actually be shopping around for the company and the particular organization they wish to join, just as they would a church. Am I saying you need to be religious in order to be in networking? Does that deserve an answer?

## I Would Bottle and Sell It

If you and I could figure out what type personality does best in this business, we could bottle that mixture and sell it and get rich. You see, many people may look good, act good, and smell good, but for some reason they just never get it together. Maybe it's a status problem. Maybe it's fear of failure. If you could just see inside them.

Another time you'll meet some shy lady in a print dress who works 9:00 to 5:00 and doesn't own a stick of furniture because she put three children through college. She decides to build the business and does. You just can't tell what beats inside a person's bosom that makes them do this business or not do it.

If a person is a good person when he or she gets into the business, chances are he or she will become a better person.

If a person is a crook, chances are he'll just become a bigger crook. You know the story of the diamond in the rough. The owner took it to a jeweler to have it polished, and asked if he could stay and watch. After it was polished, a large crack was exposed. The owner said, "The polishing made it crack." The jeweler said, "The crack was there all along. The polishing just exposed it."

## Can a Person Steal From You in This Business?

At the distributor level, there is little opportunity for a person to steal from you, since all transactions are "pay as you go." No credit.

If you are dealing with an unscrupulous company, the corporate level is a horse of a different color. If the company is less than two years old, expect the worst and hope for the best. Network marketing is the only business where the most disparaging comment you can make about a company is to say that it's new.

Imagine this scenario: The XYZ Network Company is almost two years old. The company president, knowing all along what is going to happen, lays the following trap. The company structures its bonuses so that if you are a hotshot salesman or recruiter and can put all your distributors on the front line, you could make a lot of money and get out of there quickly. They tell you that if you'll do this and that, in about a year you'll be making one hundred thousand dollars a month. But in the meantime, you won't make much.

Now let's assume there are three outstanding individuals, all with good intentions, abilities, and desires, who take the bait. They've built their organizations, and now it is time for them to start drawing the one hundred thousand dollars a month. They've told everyone.

The bonus checks are two months late, and the individuals are too embarrassed to tell their friends when the first one didn't arrive or bounced.

By the end of the second month, when the third check is due, they run to the fancy headquarters and wait in the lobby and discuss the situation with one another. The president of the company tells them, "We've built too fast and are overextended." He cons them and their individual friends into going to the bank to get an $11 million loan to pay back bonuses. The president, with the $600,000 in back bonuses, plus the new $11 million, files Chapter 11, telling them it wasn't enough to bail them out. He steals away into the night to the next state, to work his magic again.

This story is legion. Only the name of the company, the label on the product, and the location of the corporate headquarters change. The characters stay the same.

Do you see that just for a company to survive five years is a big plus? It's not everything, but it is a big plus.

## No Shows

I love "no shows." It's the only time I get to eat or visit with and train the distributor whose prospect didn't show up. If you are showing the plan for your company several times a day, it doesn't matter. I book every slot during a given time frame, and then I double-book it with another distributor at the same coffee shop. The distributor who is bringing the prospect to look at the business cannot control whether or not his prospect comes. How he invites him will have to do with whether or not the person shows up. But I expect the distributor to be there, whether or not his prospect is. He *can* control his own actions.

## Distributors Who Don't Show

If the distributor I am helping doesn't show up for the appointment (I don't tell him this in advance), I immediately move him over to my group recruiting and training sessions. No longer do I work with him individually, other than for unusual exceptions. It's my time, and I can give it anywhere I want. I won't allow him to prostitute my talents but once. Maybe twice. Before I make it firm, I ask him or her if he or she has listened to the first four training tapes. If not, I have a little more evidence that I am whipping a dead horse. From the Bible we read, "Don't cast your pearls before swine." A little harsh? Use your own judgment. That's my best thinking on the subject.

They don't have to buy the four tapes, and they don't have to listen to them. But the four tapes teach them four aspects of the business that gives us a basis upon which to build. It's not much fun for a good tennis player to play with someone who doesn't even have a racket and has never hit a ball. It's not likely that a pro tennis player is going to play with someone to whom he has to lend a racket or who has never seen one. I decided early that, because I didn't have to do this business, if I couldn't have fun with it, I wouldn't do it at all.

I am not saying you shouldn't be serious and treat this as a business; if you are going to build a big networking business, you'll have to become as serious as a heart attack. But I think you can be serious and have fun, too. Part of having fun is being with people you like. If you find an arrogant rascal, you don't have to work with him. Find someone in your downline who likes working with arrogant rascals. I don't have many who like that type. Do you?

There are not many absolutes in this business, but here is one: You may come into this business hardhearted and thin-skinned, but if you survive, you will develop a soft heart, a thick skin, and a love of people.

# Coda

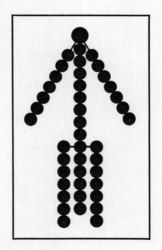

# Eighteen

# Where Else
# But in America?

W ell, we've chopped a lot of cotton. I promised you we'd get back to the story about Frog Pond Holler and the Waldorf-Astoria. Do you remember where we were? Oh, yes. I was standing there, looking over the balustrade.

As I stood there dreaming in the Waldorf, I wondered, *Where else but in America could such a dream even come true?* For a kid who got his first toys from the city dump to even be standing there. . . . Where else but in America, and what other business could afford you that opportunity with less than a hundred dollar investment?

### A Banner of Love

All I ever wanted was a chance. Perhaps that's you, too. I don't know whether or not you can build a networking business. Someone far more successful and important than I said, "Most of all, you don't know whether or not you can."

It's something you might want to make a run at. When I first saw the business, I saw it instantly. I saw that I could build a dynasty with a banner of free enterprise in one hand and a banner of love in the other. I haven't changed my mind.

## The Cutting Edge

These concepts are on the cutting edge, like a composer who experiments with dodecaphonic music and seldom ever ventures back into tertian or traditional harmony. Once a distributor has delved into Team Sponsoring and the Seven-Deep Concept, it is unlikely he will ever go back to the traditional concept.

I don't think we've touched even the "hem of the garment" in networking. Look at the possibilities of using the computer, direct mail, the telephone, and so forth. We've got to stop bowing to the sacred cow of traditional marketing concepts and get out of the buggy-whip mentality.

There is no stopping an idea whose time has come. Likewise, there is little excitement in going back to an archaic idea. I referred earlier to a song that asked, "How ya gonna keep 'em down on the farm, after they've seen Paree?"

I don't want to go back to the Model T. I want to keep the jet.

I saw a sign in a restaurant once that said, "Anyone can count the seeds in an apple, but only God can count the apples in a seed." You plant the seed from an apple and get a tree. Plant the seed from the tree and get an orchard. Plant the seed from the orchard and get . . . a dynasty.

Who was the French painter who said, "I dream my paintings and paint my dreams"? You have to understand this one fact: Your entire network empire is already out there in existence. They just haven't been contacted yet and don't know to call you.

Imagine that. Your entire Diamondship, Crown Ambassador-ship, or Presidency is intact. When you get a picture of that fixed in your mind, you will run to your next coffee shop meeting and work with a burn and a zeal that you never knew you possessed, because now you know where and how to work. Build three legs seven-deep and clone yourself in each leg. You'll run and not grow weary, because every nerve in your body will rise to the occasion. "When you're on the go, you've got the glow," and people will join you because you are going somewhere and you know where you are going and how to get there.

God bless you.

Go for it.

You can do it.

*Attacca.*

# Postlude

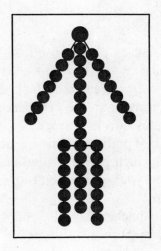

# Nineteen

# To Be Continued

In college I sold Bibles door-to-door. At sales school they taught us two things:

1. Any fool can criticize, and most fools do.

2. A wise man learns from the experience of others; a fool ought to learn from his own experience.

I suppose the highest praise for what we are doing came from a person with a very high pin in our business. He said, "I'm going to tell everyone your system won't work and go home and teach it to my group."

I believe it was Abraham Lincoln who said, "I'll prepare myself and perhaps my chance will come."

To be continued. . . .